I0427746

CONTENTS

FIGURES

INTRODUCTION

THESIS

In order to deliver effective Homeland Defense/Homeland Security, the United States needs a National Security Structure, which facilitates unity of purpose. Achieving unity of purpose, however, will require extensive government reform and national security organizational restructuring, led by the office of the President. If reform is not accomplished there will be <u>dire consequences</u>!

Approach to the topic

This analysis scrutinizes the problem of national security (NS) or more specifically the provision of Homeland Security (HS) within the NS paradigm. The conclusion of this thesis is drawn from research of the differing aspects of Homeland Security/Homeland Defense(HS/HD), the agencies or organizations charged with those duties, the existing individual and joint policy guidance under which they operate and recommendations for reform to correct any systemic deficiencies.

This thesis begins by introducing the subject of Homeland Security and providing a background synopsis. Chapter 1 explores the terminology associated with Homeland Security/Homeland Defense (HS/HD) taken from doctrine and law, in order to display the confusion which multiple definitions and overlapping direction causes. Chapter 2 examines prescient national security threats, focusing primarily on terrorism. Threat examination assists in determining if the organization providing homeland security correctly bases its duties on identification of the problem or its statutory assignment of duties. Chapter 3 analyzes the primary agencies charged with HS/HD duties, exposing the strengths, weaknesses, opportunities and threats facing the agencies or organizations

1

charged with those duties and the confusion resulting from jurisdictional and mission overlap. Evaluation and study of the various recommendations for reform of the National Security System in Chapter 4 point the way toward a suggested course of action and illumination of a possible systemic deficit. Lastly, in Chapters 5 and 6 the recommendations and conclusions presented demonstrate the need for a synergistic solution to protect the homeland. This thesis concentrates on solutions related to the addressing the counter-terrorism threat due to its imminence as a national threat and to further illustrate the need for primacy of concern on the issue of counter-terrorism.

The terrorist attacks of September 11, 2001 (9/11) demonstrated that bureaucratic infighting and the lack of information sharing, intelligence fusion, and resource efficiency costs American lives[1]. Although joint doctrine for inter-agency and DoD HD operations currently exists it does not assure effective operations. The complexity of combating current threats creates questions regarding its effectiveness and applicability.

A study completed by the Center for Strategic and International Studies (CSIS) entitled *Beyond Goldwater-Nichols: Defense Reform for a New Strategic Era* examined and reported on the paradigm shift required to effect a viable and effective, ―whole of government‖ approach to the National Security problem[2]. The Project for National Security Reform (PNSR) [3] conducted by The Center for the Study of the Presidency also suggests comprehensive reform actions to produce a wide-ranging national security

---

[1] Peter D. Buck. *The Iranian Hostage Rescue Attempt: A Case Study*. Quantico, Va: U.S. Marine Corps Command and Staff College, 2002. This footnote refers to the failed hostage retrieval of Desert One. Peter Buck‗s case study is an examination of the systemic dysfunction of the failed mission.

[2] Clark A.Murdock, and Richard W. Weitz. 2005. "Beyond Goldwater--Nichols." *JFQ: Joint Force Quarterly* no. 38: 34-41. *Academic Search Premier*, EBSCO*host* (accessed March 27, 2010).

[3] James R. Locher III, et al., *Project on National Security Reform: Turning Ideas Into Action*, Center for the Study of the Presidency (Arlington, VA, 2009).

solution for the homeland. While the foregoing presented evidence that demonstrates primacy of the problem and feasible solutions, the question of reform implementation remains. Why has the United States government failed to implement suggested reform recommendations?

National Security reform recommendations are numerous and appear easy to implement by simply directing that process reform occur, but the fact that the U.S. government has failed to effectively address systemic deficiencies implies that reform is difficult to accomplish for other reasons. The lack of common homeland security terminology, overlapping agency authorities and missions, and an increasing variety of emerging threats, when balanced against political and agency resistance to change, equate to a mammoth, if not impossible, reform task. The evidence found while researching this thesis revealed the daunting complexity of the national security problem and the absolute need for executive level intervention and direction. Presidential-led priority reform of national security including organizational restructuring that delineates specific duties and responsibilities will provide America, Homeland Defense and Homeland Security that works. If reform is the solution; the question, which leads to that conclusion, remains unanswered: ―Who does what, and to whom, in the day to day management of Homeland Security?"

Is national security, homeland defense? Is homeland defense the same as homeland security? Are these terms interchangeable? Does Homeland Security begin with foreign actors planning acts that have detrimental effects on U.S. soil or affect U.S. national interests? These seemingly, simple questions require complex solutions. These questions also demonstrate a confusing predicament for national security; imagine the organizational confusion of attempting to disarm the proverbial, ticking bomb with no knowledge of who has it, what type it is, where it may detonate, and who else is working on which part of disarming it. That ambiguous set of circumstances is the daily paradigm under which HS operates, until a significant event occurs. Following a catastrophic event, domestic incident management is coordinated by DHS under the National Response Framework (NRF) protocols, which are discussed in later chapters.

In customary nation-state paradigms, acknowledged forms of aggression are aimed at elements of national power: diplomatic, informational, military, and economical (DIME). They are also acts, which precede or are active elements of warfare. In recent years, the character of war has evolved and now includes irregular threats, which include acts of violence by both military and non-military actors. Oftentimes, these non-nation/state extremists act in non-conventional, kinetic ways to achieve their objectives. These extremists use the element of terrorism directed at non-combatant populations to stimulate terror and panic. Terrorism is an element of IW and its basis can be the furtherance of power, anarchy, religious zealotry, or economic gain. The concept of terrorism within (IW) now reveals new faces of extremist actors on the national security threat stage. Terrorism's newest actors can be domestic or internationally based and are not bound by the same paradigms as nation-state military forces. Per the theories of Prussian strategy theorist Carl Von Clausewitz, ―War is thus an act of force to compel our enemy to do our will."[4] What happens then, when non-state actors, non-military or U.S. citizens perform acts of violence to impose their will or adversely affect national

---

[4] Carl von Clausewitz, *On War, ed* -Michael Howard, and Peter Paret. New York and Toronto: Alfred A. Knopf, 1993, 83.

elements of power? Are these actors considered criminals or combatants? Transnational terrorism, anarchy, cyber attacks and transnational crime have opened new questions of jurisdiction, authority, detention and deterrence for the HS community. The narco-terrorism threat is also growing exponentially, crossing the borders between countries and crossing the jurisdictions between agencies with counter-terrorism (CT) and counter-narcotics (CN) enforcement missions. Current military defense and civilian HS organizational structures are too hierarchical and do not lend themselves to resource or information sharing. Collaboration and cooperation in all national security segments from planning through tactical response is the most pressing, practical manner to address the limitations, which prevent effective comprehensive security of the homeland.

The Department of Homeland Security (DHS) realizes that the agency cannot focus on a single entity or terrorist element; the threats are too numerous, too volatile and they do not begin or end at the U.S. border. DHS Secretary Janet Napolitano stated, "We monitor the risks of violent extremism taking root here in the United States. We don't have the luxury of focusing our efforts on one group; we must protect the country from terrorism whether foreign or homegrown, and regardless of the ideology that motivates its violence."[5]

If Secretary Napolitano's comment reflects a correct assumption, the protection of America begins with a designated agency or agencies responsible for it and includes the cooperation of the HS community of interest to protect America. As it pertains to this

---

[5] U.S. Department of Homeland Security. *Statement by U.S. Department of Homeland Security Secretary Janet Napolitano on the Threat of Right-Wing Extremism,* Janet Napolitano, Office of the Press Secretary for the Department of Homeland Security, (Washington D.C.,2009).

thesis, there can be no boundary between Homeland Security and Homeland Defense. In order to make an informed conclusion, the events, actions, roles, and responsibilities that led to the current state of Homeland Security are further explored to bear out the reform requirement and the need for Presidential-led change.

Background

"We have some planes. Just stay quiet, and you'll be O.K. We are returning to the airport."

Transmission received from American Airlines Flight 11 at 8:24 am, September 11, 2001[6].

The words —W *have some planes…"* heard by the FAA's Boston Center are arguably the beginning of a change in America's history, which should never be forgotten. On September 11, 2001, extremist Muslims in the name of jihad, inflicted violence upon United States (U.S.) soil in a coordinated attack using hijacked commercial airliners. The 9/11attacks resulted in the creation of a new security structure with far-reaching capabilities, enhanced authorities and integrated efforts to protect the American Homeland or did it? The National Security Act of 1947[7] as amended in 1949, 1953 and again in 1958 until its aim was rejuvenated by the legislation of the Goldwater-Nichols Act of 1986, is the origin of national security reform in America. The Act illustrates initial attempts to direct military and inter-agency (IA) joint-ness through reform and restructure of the U.S. national security machine. The gist of both efforts was the melding of DoD and the inter-agency (IA) into a collective effort that provided clear lines

---

[6] *FAA audio file, Boston Center, position 46R, 8:24:38 and 8:24:56; Peter Zalewski interview (Sept. 23, 2003* of: *The 9/11 Commission Report: Final Report of the National Commission on Terrorist Attacks Upon the United States.* New York: Norton, 2004, as cited on pages 10 and 455.

[7] National Security Act of 1947." *National Security Act of 1947* (January 17, 2009): 1. *Academic Search Premier*, EBSCO*host* (accessed March 27, 2010).

of DoD command authority and set the stage for economy of effort, in defending America.

The Act's purpose was to unify military and IA efforts in order to provide comprehensive readiness and threat awareness to U.S. national security efforts; however, it did not. No one perceived the threat of "irregular warfare" on U.S. soil until the morning of September 11, 2001. America's power projection in the form of major combat operations (MCO) had historically occurred overseas and had failed to appropriately plan for acts of violence domestically. The DoD paradigm in a world where terrorist acts were increasing in both numbers and violence did not prepare the homeland for a sneak attack by non-state actors. <u>Being unprepared did not mean being unaware, it simply implied there was a failure to act preemptively in order to avoid a domestic attack.</u> DoD assets lacked situational awareness, domestic authority and jurisdictional ability to act in preventing the 9/11 terrorist attacks; it simply was not DoD's job. At the time of the attacks the Department of Homeland Security (DHS) did not exist and there was not in place a coordinated national security mechanism to provide protection for the homeland. If the restructuring of the defensive arm of national security (DoD) only provided for defense of the homeland from abroad, how then is domestic protection of the homeland structured and implemented?

Born out of the aftermath of the worst terrorist attack on U.S. soil thus far, the Department of Homeland Security (DHS) created by the Homeland Security Act of 2002[8]

---

[8] *Homeland Security Act of 2002*. Stat2135, Washington, D.C.: U.S. Government Printing Office, 2002. 116.

(HSA), combined 22 agencies to provide domestic national security. DHS protects U.S. soil from the introduction of dangerous persons or materials and has responsibility for the integration, coordination, planning, response and recovery efforts related to catastrophic events. As with any evolving agency, DHS is not without controversy both internally and externally. The diverse efforts, fight for resources, jurisdictional issues, applications of law and lack of unified efforts among entities responsible for homeland security resulted in a cacophony of confusion. Each government agency has its own equities in providing HS, often jurisdictions overlap and in some cases, the fight for the media spotlight as a means to increase budgets outweighs the efficacy of a unified effort. Examples such as determining when acts of terrorism (DoJ/DHS) become acts of war (DOD/DoS) or who is criminal (DoJ/DHS/ODNI) or enemy combatant (DoD) during commission of a domestic terrorist act as an IW statement come to mind.

Do we use the criminal justice system or military tribunals to prosecute participants in terrorist acts? Arguments regarding terrorist prosecutions continue about the associated costs, public safety from retribution, the span of punishments available to impose and the rights granted suspects under each system. The Department of Justice's (DoJ)'s planned 2010 prosecution of Khalid Sheikh Mohammed, (the accused chief architect of the 9/11 attacks) and four accomplices in NYC is the object of such contention. The resistance of New York City (NYC) official's is due to high cost projections and perceived danger to the public with the city as the venue of the trial. Officials and the public are also in opposition on the proposed trial's Manhattan location within view of the 9/11 crime scene site, seen by some as an affront to the memory of the fallen. Various other factors such as court jurisdiction, hyper-alert public sentiment, and

8

vulnerability to retaliatory attacks are significant in making the final decision of prosecuting terrorists under the criminal justice system or military tribunal. Application of the law is not clear-cut on this issue, which leads to more confusion and illustrates gaps and seams in the HS structure.

The U.S. Government's (USG) national interest is reflected in use of the public platform of the American justice system to mete out lawful prosecution and punishment for acts of violence perpetrated against U.S. citizens or interests. On the world stage, the strategic communication requirement is for America to demonstrate that even under extreme, visceral and dire circumstances everyone receives due process. This is a situation where national interests conflict with state interests; clearly national interest are in line with diplomatic or political posturing and state objectives are self-protective. Gaps and seams in the prosecution paradigm are the result of rapid implementation of plans and processes in direct response to the 9/11 attacks.

Reform drives the development of cogent structure, and efficient mechanisms to manage risk from origin through resolution, in this case, resolution being trial by military tribunal or the criminal justice system. N/S reform incorporates the needed elements of law, applicability, and refined processes to cover gaps in the judicial system and facilitate lawful prosecution.

The holistic nature of National Security reform in the legislative arena of HS/HD provides answers to the question of who is responsible for prosecuting terrorists and under which system, by developing and implementing a new NS Act, which encompasses a holistic structure to address a massively complex problem. The public demands justice for the spilled blood of the innocents, fiscal responsibility for the best use of resources is part of the public trust and fairness in prosecution, and punishment must be the result of America living up to its justice and human rights creed in all aspects of HS.

Initially, the question was at what point does NS/HS and HD intersect? The broad duties and fundamental elements of each term and discipline are synonymous with the goal of protecting America. The goal of comprehensive HS must be strategic in scope and directive in nature, present in the national strategy, and reflected in the succeeding agency strategies that evolve from it. The National Security Strategy for Homeland Security (NSHS) provides a framework for the nation's goals and communicates U.S. grand strategy contained within the National Security Strategy of the United States. Chapter 1 will begin with a review of the terminology within such documents to provide insight into NS/HS/HD commonalities related to the strategic goal of National Security.

CHAPTER 1

HOMELAND SECURITY – AN EXAMINATION OF TERMS

The *U.S. Department of Homeland Security Strategic Plan Fiscal Years 2008–2013*[1] does not include a definition of Homeland Security (HS), National Security (NS), or Homeland Defense (HD); it does however, enumerate key functional areas that facilitate the strategic objectives of the Department of Homeland Security (DHS) strategy, which are key to an all-inclusive security approach. Appendix I contains a synopsis of DHS functionalities derived from a review of the DHS Strategic Plan. Although the DHS Strategic Plan functionalities do not represent comprehensive definitions, they relate the core competencies addressed by DHS efforts to provide comprehensive Homeland Security. The functionality areas synopsized in Appendix I are: intelligence fusion[2], border security and transportation protection, domestic terrorism, critical infrastructure and key resource protection, weapons of mass destruction (WMD) and, emergency preparedness and continuity of government.

Effective organizations may view NS mission objectives from differing perspectives but all require a basis in a common understanding of terminology. Differing definitions of the same term can lead to different interpretations and result in a variety of efforts, varying perceptions, inefficiency, and confusion as to the desired end state. Homeland Security is inclusive of numerous disciplines, efforts, missions and

---

[1] United States. *One Team, One Mission, Securing Our Homeland U.S. Department of Homeland Security Strategic Plan, Fiscal Years 2008-2013*. Washington, D.C.: The Department, 2008. 6-36.

[2] This thesis avoids extensive analysis of HS/HD intelligence deficiencies, as they are not within the proposed scope of this thesis.

organizations with diverse definitions contained in their doctrine and policy. In order to appreciate the confusion surrounding HS, further examination of common terminology available in doctrine and law are explored to provide a universal understanding. As a definition is not present in DHS's strategic guidance, other documentation pertaining to National Security or Homeland Defense may reveal a clearer meaning.

Defining Homeland Security

Renowned essayist, G.K. Chesterton once remarked, ―It isn't that they can't see the solution. It's that they can't see the problem."[3] Chesterton was right, and defining a problem is the first step toward finding a solution. If the foundation for action lies in doctrine or policy then foundational documents should have common terminology. Situational awareness aspects such as a common operating picture, common intelligence picture, or the idea of a common perspective are gained through common starting points. The expectation is that the singular definition of HS or HD begins with the National Security Strategy (NSS) pointing the way towards a final objective of effective National Security. The most current NSS document is dated March 2006.

United States National Security Strategy (NSS). At the time of this writing, the current National Security Strategy (NSS) of the United States has no definition for Homeland Security, Homeland Defense or National Security.[4] The NSS and the speeches and directives of the President provide the national vision or grand strategy of the U.S.

---

[3] 2010 Famous Quotes and Authors.com. http://www famousquotesandauthors.com/ authors/g__k__chesterton_quotes.html (accessed 1 April 2010).

[4] United States. *The National Security Strategy of the United States of America*. President of the U.S., (Washington D.C.: 2002).

providing context and direction for the application of elements of national power to provide safety, security, and prosperity for America. The grand strategy resident in the current NSS appears to be included in the two pillars espoused by President George Bush: "promoting freedom, justice, and human dignity" and "leading and expanding democracy throughout the world." The global commons upon which we all depend require defense of liberty to ensure its propagation. The current NSS does not clearly denote a path toward comprehensive NS.

Following the Sept 11, 2001 attacks, and the establishment of the Homeland Security Advisory Council (HSAC), the initial definition of Homeland Security as stated in the initial Strategic Plan for Homeland Security provided by the White House Office of Homeland Security read as follows, "Homeland Security is a concerted national effort to prevent terrorist attacks within the United States, reduce America's vulnerability to terrorism, and minimize the damage and recover from attacks that do occur."[5]

Clearly, the previous definition is based on the counter-terrorism response to the 9/11 attacks. The definition addresses terrorism but is not comprehensive. The HS definition was then expanded and the duties in the updated National Response Plan (NRP) are a result of the direction in Homeland Security Presidential Directive-5 (HSPD-5). Under HSPD-5, President Bush directed development of the (NRP) to align federal coordination structures, capabilities, and resources into a unified, all discipline, and all

---

[5] Homeland Security Council (U.S.), and United States. *National Strategy for Homeland Security.* The White House (Washington, D.C.: 2002). 2.

hazards approach to domestic incident management[6]. The HSPD-5 document begins to shape the definition of HS as domestic incident management only.

The HS *Initial National Response Plan* (INRP)[7], document speaks to DHS's duties as management of domestic incidents while adding the elements of major disasters and other emergencies to the definition:

> Management of Domestic Incidents establishes clear objectives for a concerted national effort to prevent terrorist attacks within the United States; reduce America's vulnerability to terrorism, major disasters, and other emergencies; and minimize the damage and recover from attacks, major disasters, and other emergencies that occur.[8]

Interpreted to fall into these areas of ―other emergencies" are the missions associated with disaster recovery, emergency preparedness and response as well as continuity of government and national resilience. From its creation, the DHS role in managing domestic response was defined and limited to the domestic area of responsibility (AOR).

Homeland Security Act of 2002 (HSA): It is perplexing to realize that the legislative act that created the Department of Homeland Security following the attacks of September 11 does not define HS until the section for budgetary classification, wherein it states the following:

> (B) In this paragraph, consistent with the Office of Management and Budget's June 2002 ‗Annual Report to Congress on Combating Terrorism', the term ‗homeland security' refers to those activities that

---

[6] George W. Bush. Homeland Security Presidential Directive-5. "Directive on Management of Domestic Incidents." *Weekly Compilation of Presidential Documents* 39, no. 10: 280. Pages 1 and 2. *Academic Search Premier.* Washington D.C.: 2003.EBSCO*host* (accessed March 27, 2010).

[7] United States. *National Response Plan,* Dept. of Homeland Security (Washington DC: 2004).1.

[8] Ibid. 1.

detect, deter, protect against, and respond to terrorist attacks occurring within the United States and its territories[9].

Referencing HS as a budgetary concern lent credibility for the urgency of funding based on America's need to exact retribution and ensure that terrorist acts on U.S. soil would not happen again. The myriad legislative acts that created and reorganized the Inter-Agency (IA) following 9/11 also produced a new agency; the Department of Homeland Security (DHS) with broad powers and federal organizations all merged into an effort to provide protection for the homeland. DHS as an agency is further discussed in Chapter 3 of this thesis. Legislative action swift and powerful enough to ensure the level of protection expected of DHS had to be Presidential directed.

Homeland Security Presidential Directive-1(HSPD-1): HSPD-1created the Homeland Security Council (HSC) and enumerated its functions. The HSC provides executive level advice to the President concerning HS policy for coordinating homeland security-related efforts across executive departments and agencies and at all levels of government and private business throughout the country. The HSC is also charged with the duty to implement national HS policies throughout the HS community of interest (COI).[10] HSPD-1 astonishingly, does not define NS/HS/or HD! DHS as an organization continues to grow and change, following in the example of its predecessor; the Department of Defense, DHS reviewed its processes and policies in order to improve its

---

[9] *Homeland Security Act of 2002*. Stat: 2251. U.S. Government Printing Office (Washington, D.C.:2002). 116. This part of the Act refers to the HS funding analysis in the President's budget and provides definition of HS function.

[10] George W. Bush. Homeland Security Presidential Directive-1. *Organization and Operation of the Homeland Security Council*. HSPD-1. The White House (Washington, D.C.: 2001).Per HSPD-1 President Bush established the HSC and delineated its duties.

statutory performance. Organizational review processes such as the quadrennial review system are one such manner to accomplish the task of internal analysis and external effectiveness.

DHS Quadrennial Homeland Security Review (QHSR): The DHS Quadrennial Homeland Security Review released in February 2010 discusses the new paradigm under which DHS is evolving. As quoted from the QHSR document: ―Homeland Security describes the intersection of evolving threats and hazards with the transitional governmental and civic responsibilities of civil defense, emergency response, law enforcement, customs, border control and immigration."[11]

The QHSR's definition is placed at the end of the section seeking a common definition for HS, as it is the most recent and most visionary. DHS recognizes the comprehensiveness of the HS task and the required collective solution. The QHSR adds to the HS lexicon the phrase ―homeland security enterprise" as the overarching model for not just a ―whole of government" solution but a ―U.S. and its people" solution. The ―enterprise" concept represents a totality of efforts from the HS community of interest to share resources, information, capabilities, and capacities in order to realize the return of the safe and secure mindset to America.

Homeland Defense (HD) is the DoD paradigm for defining the intersect of HS and HD mission, not necessarily limited to domestic actions. The next section examines the DoD characterizations of the HD definition.

---

[11] U.S. Government, Department of Homeland Security, *Quadrennial Homeland Security Review Report,* Janet Napolitano DHS Press Room, ii. (Washington D.C. February 2010).

Defining Homeland Defense

National Security Act of 1947 (NSA): The NS Act does not define HS, possibly because the concept did not exist during the Act's inception. National Security was the watchword of the day in 1947 and Soviet aggression was the primary threat at the time of the NSA's implementation. The verbiage outlined in the Act as follows demonstrates the integration of the comprehensive duties of the Committee on Transnational Threats and defines the threat:

(4) In carrying out its function, the Committee shall

(A) Identify transnational threats;

(B) Develop strategies to enable the United States Government to respond to transnational threats identified under subparagraph (A);

(C) Monitor implementation of such strategies;

(D) Make recommendations as to appropriate responses to specific transnational threats;

(E) Assist in the resolution of operational and policy differences among Federal departments and agencies in their responses to transnational threats;

(F) Develop policies and procedures to ensure the effective sharing of information about transnational threats among Federal departments and agencies, including law enforcement agencies and the elements of the intelligence community; and

(G) Develop guidelines to enhance and improve the coordination of activities of Federal law enforcement agencies and elements of the intelligence community outside the United States with respect to transnational threats.

(5) For purposes of this subsection, the term "transnational threat" means the following:

(A) Any transnational activity (including international terrorism, narcotics trafficking, the proliferation of weapons of mass destruction and the delivery systems for such weapons, and organized crime) that threatens the national security of the United States.

(B) Any individual or group that engages in an activity referred to in subparagraph (A).[12]

The National Security Act of 1947 created the National Security Council (NSC) and charged it with the integration of domestic, foreign, and military policy as well as integration and facilitation of cooperative relationships between DoD and other departments. Surprisingly the NSC established the Committee on Transnational Threats that in effect became a mini-DHS per its duties, which included combating terrorism, countering transnational threats and narcotics trafficking as well as counter-proliferation of-weapons of mass destruction (WMD). The committee's transnational threat duties practically mirror DoD/DHS/DoJ current counter-terrorism HS functions.

National Defense Strategy (NDS): The National Defense Strategy (NDS) under the section, <u>Defend the Homeland</u> simply describes the DoD HD duties as follows: ―The core responsibility of the Department of Defense is to defend the United States from attack upon its territory at home and to secure its interests abroad."[13] The responsibilities enumerated in the NDS infer universal duties covering both internal and external defense. Core responsibility however, does not dictate primary leadership in HS/HD matters.

National Military Strategy (NMS): The National Military Strategy (NMS) addresses defensive domestic efforts under the section marked as Domestic Actions at Home:

---

[12] National Security Act of 1947." *National Security Act of 1947* (January 17, 2009): 1. *Academic Search Premier*, EBSCO*host* (accessed March 27, 2010).

[13] United States. *National Defense Strategy*, Department of Defense, (Washington D.C.: 2008). 6.

While we will attempt to counter threats close to their source and interdict them along the strategic approaches, we must retain the ability to defend the United States from an attack that penetrates our forward defenses. At home the Armed Forces must defend the United States against air and missile attacks, terrorism and other direct attacks.[14]

The NMS speaks to the strategic ability to incorporate defense-in-depth, since earliest opportunity for counter-threat operations begins at threat origin and ends at resilience and recovery on U.S. soil if OCONUS efforts fail. U.S. Information Operations (IO) must now target ideological methodologies as a means to squelch threats in the earliest recruitment phases. This process is especially important when considering sympathetic recruitment of indigenous populations to become homegrown terrorists.

National Security Presidential Directive-1(NSPD-1): NSPD-1, implemented pre-9/11, under the Bush Administration does not address Homeland Security but does address National Security interests. NSPD-1 champions America's safety by way of securing the democracy and its advancement in keeping with the pillars of the National Security Strategy: ―National security includes the defense of the United States of America, protection of our constitutional system of government, and the advancement of United States interests around the globe."[15]

Joint doctrine includes definitions for both HD and HS and includes the DHS National Response Framework definition. Included below are excerpts from joint doctrine documents that recognize the gap between the two concepts.

---

[14] United States. *The National Military Strategy of the United States of America: A Strategy for Today, a Vision for Tomorrow,* 10. Joint Chiefs of Staff, (Washington, D.C.: 2004).10.

[15] United States. *The National Security Strategy of the United States of America.* President of the U.S. (Washington D.C.: 2002).

DoD Joint Operating Concept 3-08, (V-2), DoD Joint Publication 3-27-Homeland Defense, and DoD Joint Publication 3-28-Civil Support all include the same definition for HD and HS. They are as follows:

> Homeland Defense (HD): The protection of U.S. sovereignty, territory, domestic population, and critical defense infrastructure against external threats and aggression, or other threats as directed by the President. The DOD is responsible for the strategy of HD and Civilian Support (CS)"[16]

> Homeland Security (HS): A concerted national effort to prevent terrorist attacks within the U.S. ,reduce America's vulnerability to terrorism, and minimize the damage and recover from attacks that do occur." (National Strategy for Homeland Security)[17]

> Homeland Security (HS): The Homeland is confronted with threats ranging from traditional national security threats (for example, ballistic missile attack) to law enforcement threats (for example, bank robbery). There are clear definitions of both ends and less clarity in the middle where military and civilian roles often overlap. In the middle is a ―seam" of ambiguity where threats are neither clearly national security threats (the primary responsibility of DOD) nor clearly law enforcement threats (the responsibility of the Department of Homeland Security [DHS], the Department of Justice (DOJ) or other agencies. In addition, DOD assistance may be required to mitigate the effects and manage the consequences of catastrophic events. This situation highlights the criticality of communication, coordination, and cooperation among DOD and federal, state, local, and international partners.[18]

That joint doctrine speaks to the seams and gaps left by ambiguity is important as validation of the need for a common definition to focus the scope of the desired overall end state. More importantly recognition of the ―seam of ambiguity" caused by mission

---

[16] United States. *Department of Defense Homeland Security Joint Operating Concept Version 2.0.* USNORTHCOM Strategy Division (J5S), (Peterson AFB, Colo: 2007).

[17] United States. *One Team, One Mission, Securing Our Homeland U.S. Department of Homeland Security Strategic Plan, Fiscal Years 2008-2013,* The Department, (Washington, D.C.: 2008). 6-36.

[18] Ibid,United States. *Department of Defense Homeland Security Joint Operating Concept, Version 2.0.* USNORTHCOM Strategy Division (J5S), (Peterson AFB, Colo: 2007).

overlap has to be addressed. NS reform begins with a common definition leading to a common strategy and ending with unity of purpose providing comprehensive NS.

Quadrennial Defense Review (QDR) 2006 and 2010: The DoD congressionally directed Quadrennial Defense Review occurs every four years and includes a comprehensive review of status, mission, efficacy, policy, training, acquisition and doctrine of the force. The 2006 QDR addresses Homeland Defense in terms of steady state and surge conditions:

> Defend the Homeland Steady state, detect, deter, and if necessary, defeat external threats to the U.S. homeland, and enable partners to contribute to U.S. national security. Examples of such activities include: routine homeland security training and exercises with other Federal agencies and state and local governments; strategic deterrence; routine maritime operations conducted with the U.S. Coast Guard; North America air defense, including air sovereignty operations; missile defense; and readiness to provide support to civil authorities for consequence management events.
>
> Surge – contribute to the nation's response to and management of the consequences of WMD attacks or a catastrophic event, such as Hurricane Katrina, and also to raise the level of defense responsiveness in all domains (e.g., air, land, maritime, space and cyberspace) if directed.[19]

The 2006 QDR interpretation is consistent with DoD's propensity to frame HD in a manner consistent with its major planning concepts of contingency planning to manage long-term phased directed changes in the steady state and crisis action planning to manage surge conditions. Framing in this way provides a common organizational foundation consistent with organizational culture, processes, and planning models.

---

[19] Department of Defense, *Quadrennial Defense Review Report* (QDR), Donald Rumsfeld. (Washington D.C.: 2006). 37.

The 2010 QDR does not speak directly to what Homeland Defense means; it is characterized within the document as the capability of DoD's supporting role and its development of capacity to provide support to civil authorities in emergency preparedness and response to catastrophic events. DoD organizational paradigm shift in this direction is visionary of organizational planning to meet future challenges vice post change adaptation.

Organizations charged with providing comprehensive HS need a common foundation; this commonality improves the chance for success as multiple agencies collaborative efforts lead to the foundation of a hybrid organization to address common threats. Common definitions lead to better defined roles, responsibilities, and interconnected processes to diminish gaps and smooth seams. Reform incorporates joint and combined efforts effectively focusing elements of power into a unified effort, moving past the encumbrances of organizational equities and identities. Government agencies traditionally develop institutional cultural identities. Failing to curtail agency identities for the common good creates barriers to unified efforts within unified organizations (commands). Suppressing predominant agency identities usually occurs through hierarchal mandate or legislative direction. Agency equities can, however, be preserved within the totality of the overall mission, as with joint efforts like Joint Inter-Agency Task Force (JIATF)-South or U.S. Special Operations Command's (SOCOM) Interagency Task Force (IATF). Within the NS structure, agency equity preservation and organizational efficacy is still achievable when the overarching goal and not the individual agency goal remains the universal focus.

The lack of definitions for HS/HD in doctrine and law as exemplified in leading guidance such as the NSS or NSHS, QDR, and PSD, promotes myriad interpretations demonstrating that a common reference is difficult to achieve. There are commonalities within HS/HD strategic objectives but a single framework to manage efforts is absent. Without a common definition, the final goal obscures. The desired end state or goal emanates from the stimulus requiring some sort of action. The stimulus requiring action equates to identifying the problem and the HS problem is the imminent evolving threat.

Reverse engineering from resolution through effect to cause is a process for exploration. The resolution is successful provision of HS, the effect is a comprehensive, persistent mechanism projecting that HS posture, and the cause is an emerging and adaptive threat. Exploration of the prescient threats to U.S. security may provide the context for deciding which organization or structure is responsible for homeland security.

CHAPTER 2

THE THREAT

Prior to 9/11, many believed the Continental United States (CONUS) and its territories were not a prime focus for attack; however, there are a plethora of threats that must be addressed by today's combined arms joint forces and the NS structure. The traditional mission of U.S. forces has been to address threats to U.S. national security or interests at the source outside the continental United States (OCONUS). The use of military assets for combat actions on two separate battlefronts, the support of developing democratic governments in multiple arenas, assistance in combating transnational criminal enforcement at U.S. borders, and counterterrorism response all serve to tie up elements of national power, deplete resources and distract focus from increasing danger.

Overseas Contingency Operations (OCO) and Foreign Internal Defense (FID)

The U.S. Government has engaged in the hunt for terrorists and those who would harbor them in operations such as Desert Storm/Desert Shield. The search for illicit Weapons of Mass Destruction (WMD's) and the liberation of Kuwait from a despot also embedded the influence of Western democracy on Iraq and Afghanistan populations. In furtherance of U.S. objectives to root out terrorism abroad, the U.S. Government has committed to the provision of aid and civil assistance in both countries as well as, Pakistan to include continuing actions to eliminate terrorist havens, restore government, reconstruct infrastructure and build nation capacity.

The purpose of counter-insurgency efforts of U.S. and coalition forces is to drive Taliban and Al-Qaeda from the cities and countryside of Iraq, the mountains of

Afghanistan and through the borders of Pakistan, taking away terrorist safe havens and disrupting their operations. A planned U.S. troop increase of approximately 30,000 in 2010, an assertive strategy promoting Afghan and Iraq self-sustained governments and publicly stated withdrawal plans[1] now create an impetus for increased activity by Taliban and Al-Qaeda extremists.[2] Instead of producing a ―wait it out‖ reaction to the Obama administration's troop augmentation and revitalized counter insurgency strategy, what has instead occurred is an extremist Muslim reaction of increased threats and instances of continued violence. Daily news reports confirm increases in overt violence and covert actions in Iraq, Afghanistan, and Pakistan.

America's elements of national power are spread thinly in Overseas Contingency Operations (OCO) in Afghanistan, Iraq and imminently in Pakistan, as well as the nuclear proliferation watch mode with North Korea and Iran. Lastly, America is engaged in developing active safeguards against technology, economic and critical infrastructure incursions from China, all actions that utilize more of the limited capacity within the national elements of power. For the U.S. to prevail in disrupting, dismantling and destroying violent extremists, it must not just succeed in kinetic operations but with follow-on operations that prepare indigenous populations for regime change, reconstruction, security, and self-preservation. Defense forces occupied in persistent conflict leaves the homeland less protected from attack due to stretched resources.

---

[1] Barack H. Obama. *"Responsibly Ending the War in Iraq: We Will End Combat by 2010." Vital Speeches of the Day.* 75, NO. 4: 154 delivered at Camp Lejeune, North Carolina, February 27, 2009.

[2] United States. National Security Council (NSC), Interagency Policy Group. *White Paper of the Interagency Policy Group's Report on U.S. Policy Toward Afghanistan and Pakistan.* (Washington, D.C.: 2009). The document delineates the new U.S. policy for Afghanistan and Pakistan, which could in effect tie up U.S. forces perpetually for the next decade.

Foreign Internal Defense (FID) assistance provides training for a government's security forces to hasten the removal of illicit governments or reduce insurgent activity through their own improved capacity. Training indigenous forces toward self-sufficiency relieves the U.S. Government of the drain from continual duties associated with protection and maintenance of free societies. However, the successes attributed to FID missions only serve to illuminate the reactive nature of insurgents, criminals and terrorists and places western democracies in the target sights of these actors. U.S. success OCONUS translates to increased threats to the homeland, from VEOs. These threats increase as U.S. collaborative efforts to reduce insurgencies, counter narcotics proliferation and counter terrorism are becoming standard operating procedure for U.S. forces.

Counterinsurgency (COIN), Counter-Narcotics Enforcement (CNE) and Counter Terrorism (CT)

There are three offensive functions which occupy the efforts of both military and law enforcement forces: Counterinsurgency (COIN) has become the new combat paradigm in Southeast Asia regional warfare in order to disrupt and destroy insurgent efforts; Counter-narcotics enforcement (CNE) is the directed holistic response to thwart organized drug proliferation both overseas and domestically and: counter-terrorism (CT) is the totality of efforts applied to detect, prevent or if need be respond to man-made catastrophic events meant to achieve fear in the populace.

How does a government counter terrorism? To understand the terrorism threat, it must first be defined. The primary terrorist threat to the U.S. is not the same as the political or socialist ideologically based threats of the past such as Communism or Marxism. Militant extremism is often a religious-based concept that interprets violent action from spiritual dogma. A commonly accepted definition of terrorism is, ―violence or the threat of violence carried out for political purposes[3]." This definition works well to illustrate the basis for domestic terrorist acts such as the one perpetrated by anarchist Timothy McVeigh convicted in the 1995, bombing of the Alfred P. Murrah, Federal building in Oklahoma City, Oklahoma.[4]

The context from which Homeland Security draws reference, however, is better aligned with the cultural dictionary definition:

> Acts of violence committed by groups that view themselves as victimized by some notable historical wrong. Although these groups have no formal connection with governments, they usually have the financial and moral backing of sympathetic governments. Typically, they stage unexpected attacks on civilian targets, including embassies and airliners, with the aim of sowing fear and confusion...[5]

Numerous attempted terrorist events following 9/11 demonstrate that terrorist elements are resident inside the United States. The effect gained by inculcating fear, confusion, and terror in a population is the ultimate expression of will to initiate a change in behavior or actions, no matter what the underlying reason. Numerous alleged domestic terrorism attempts have occurred in the U.S. since 2001 including acts by alleged

---

[3] Random House, Inc. terrorism. Dictionary.com. *Dictionary.com Unabridged*. s.v. ―terrorism." retrieved at http://dictionary.reference.com/browse/terrorism (accessed: January 16, 2010).

[4] CNN.com/US website article, Andy Brooks and Catherine Quayle, *Terror on Trial: Timothy McVeigh executed,* December 31, 2007. McVeigh was an anarchist who perceived himself to be at war with the U.S. government. (accessed December 12, 2009)

[5] Dictionary.com. *The American Heritage® New Dictionary of Cultural Literacy. s. v.* terrorism. *Third Edition*. Houghton Mifflin Company, 2005. http://dictionary reference.com/browse/terrorism (accessed: January 16, 2010).

embedded terrorists as well as U.S. citizen converts to fanatical extremism[6]. Counter-terrorism efforts seek to identify as early as possible those agents involved in terrorist conspiracies, deny them access to America and safe havens, disrupt their plans and financial support and destroy their infrastructure, logistics and ability to carry out violence. Counter–terrorism responsibilities are dispersed throughout the U.S. Government infrastructure, but the investigative authority for terrorism lies with the Federal Bureau of Investigation (FBI)[7]. Jurisdictional disputes in crimes involving terrorism are common such as occurs when the investigation crosses borders.

Transnational and Border Threats

Transnational terrorism and transnational crime are fast becoming the same thing. The U.S. southern border with Mexico is ripe with the expectation that violence and criminal acts, which appear to suspend the rule of law in Mexico, will extend into the U.S. The former Assistant Secretary of Immigration and Customs Enforcement (ICE), Mike Garcia, stated before Congress that: ―Organizations that exploit our borders to bring in illegal aliens or drugs could, for the right amount of money, employ those same routes and networks to smuggle terrorists or weapons of mass destruction."[8] Mr. Garcia

---

[6] Federal Bureau of Investigation website, Headline Archives, The Year In Review- *A Look at FBI Cases, Part 1*, http://www.fbi.gov/page2/dec09/review_122809.html, (accessed March 02, 2009). The site highlights 10 foiled terrorist plots/suspects of 2009, many of whom were converted in the U.S.

[7] Code of Federal Regulations (CFR) 28 Ch1 (7-1-02) Edition, Section 0.85a, (Washington D.C.) The CFR delineates the lead agency investigatory authority of the FBI for acts of terrorism or acts leading to terrorism.52.

[8] Department of Homeland Security, U.S. Immigration and Customs Enforcement, Michael Garcia *Statement of Assistant Secretary Michael J. Garcia U.S. Immigration and Customs Enforcement Department of Homeland Security Before Senate Banking, Housing and Urban Affairs continued footnote #8: Committee on "9/11 Commission Report: Terrorist Financing Issues".* (Washington, D.C.: September 29, 2004).

is correct as violence in the region of the U.S. Southwest border is on the rise. A 2008 report by the International Narcotics Control Board (INCB), which monitors implementation of the United Nations drug control conventions, states that,

> The GoM has deployed more than 12,000 military troops and has employed forces from seven Government agencies, spending more than U.S. $2.5 billion in 2007 (an increase of 24 per cent over the spending level in 2006) to improve security and reduce drug-related violence. Drug cartels have responded with unprecedented violence and the number of homicide victims, including top-level federal police officers, in 2007 and 2008 has more than doubled compared with previous years, as federal intervention is taking place in states where corruption had allowed drug traffickers to operate relatively undisturbed[9].

Much like the kinetic functions of war, law enforcement must ameliorate threats in a holistic fashion or face the consequence of multiple, simultaneous battlefronts as result of success in specific areas. The border area has numerous jurisdictions at work; U.S. Customs and Border Protection (CBP) has enforcement authority at and between the U.S. borders; Immigration and Customs Enforcement (ICE) has investigational authority for crimes committed at and between the U.S. borders or that have nexus to border areas; and the Drug Enforcement Administration (DEA) is responsible for drug interdiction and counter narcotics enforcement as it pertains to the U.S. including overseas genesis of transnational criminal conduct. Enforcement missions and duty overlaps are inevitable along the border and the probability of overlooking developing threats is inevitable.

A report completed by the Congressional Research Service makes obvious the developing nexus between crime and terrorism. The report stated ―The U.S. Drug

---

[9] United Nations, International Narcotics Control Board. *Report of the International Narcotics Control Board for 2008,* United Nations. (New York: 2009). 6.

Enforcement Administration (DEA) reports that the number of designated foreign terrorist organizations (FTOs) involved in the global drug trade has jumped from 14 groups in 2003 to 18 in 2008." [10] Narcotics traffickers and terrorists have teamed up and now present a new threat that must be managed cooperatively. Further evidence of this crime to terrorism nexus can be drawn from the December 2009, Drug Enforcement Administration's (DEA) landmark arrest, and prosecution of three suspects on drug and terrorism charges. Oumar Issa, Harouna Toure, and Idriss Abelrahman were indicted on charges of conspiracy to commit acts of narco-terrorism and conspiracy to provide material support to foreign terrorist organizations. The suspects allegedly conspired to smuggle cocaine through West and North Africa in order to provide financial support to three Department of State (DoS) designated terrorist organizations: Al Qaeda, Al Qaeda in the Islamic Magreb ("AQIM"), and the Fuerzas Armadas Revolucionarias de Colombia (Revolutionary Armed Forces of Colombia or (FARC). Acting DEA Administrator Michele Leonhart stated:

> Today's arrests are further proof of the direct link between dangerous
> terrorist organizations, including Al Qaeda, and international drug
> trafficking that fuels their violent activities... These narco-terrorists do not
> respect borders and do not care who they harm with their drug trafficking
> conspiracies. [11]

These indictments mark the first time that associates of Al Qaeda have been charged with narco-terrorism offenses in the U.S. Leonhart's statement in the press release following

---

[10] United States. *Narco-Terrorism: International Drug Trafficking and Terrorism, a Dangerous Mix : Hearing Before the Committee on the Judiciary, United States Senate, One Hundred Eighth Congress, First Session, May 20, 2003*. U.S. G.P.O., (Washington, D. C.: 2003).

[11] United States, News Release, *Three Al Qaeda Associates Arrested on Drug and Terrorism Charges*. DEA Acting Administrator Michele Leonhart and United States Attorney Preet Bharara. DEA Public Affairs Office. (Washington D.C.: 2009).

the arrests cannot belie the effort it will take to continue this type of law enforcement. Crime and terrorism will keep all facets of national power busy for some time to come as Al-Qaeda and Taliban influence expands.

Al Qaeda, Taliban

Al Qaeda currently operates from safe havens along the Afghan-Pakistan border, through their strategic communications network. Their insidious network of operatives and funding is provided by both legitimate and illicit activities. This extremist group continues to present a viable threat to the U.S. and its people. To understand the motivation of extremist Muslims like Al Qaeda, is to understand the threat they pose. Al Qaeda's transnational Jihad, which focuses on the destruction and disruption of Western democracies, is the pre-eminent terrorist threat facing the U.S. The possibility of Al Qaeda's use of weapons of mass destruction (WMD) to inflict mass casualties and horrific shock is becoming a focus of international counter-terrorism efforts of the U.S. and its allies. Prior to 9/11, the U.S. Government had substantial information that violent extremist had planned attacks on U.S. soil. Al-Qaeda and Bin Laden specifically, were targets of interest by the intelligence community prior to 9/11 and remain so. The Congressional Select Committee on Intelligence conducted a joint inquiry into the activities of the U.S. Intelligence Community (IC) surrounding the 9/11 attacks and discovered that in December 1998, George Tenet, the Director of Central Intelligence, targeted Bin Laden and increased the counter-terrorism effort. George Tenet's direction to his deputies was as follows: ―We must now enter a new phase in our effort against Bin Laden…We are at war…I want no resources or people spared in this effort, either inside

31

the CIA or the Community."[12] Despite the passion of Tenet's direction, the increased efforts and targeting of the IC, 9/11 still occurred and the growth of violent Muslim ideology has continued. Couple the terrorist group's growth with the use of coercion and inducement, or subornation of underprivileged populations such as occurs in Afghanistan, Pakistan, Yemen or Iraq with the inducement and indoctrination training of Muslim converts located in America and the question is no longer <u>if more catastrophic attacks on U.S. soil will occur, but when will they occur?</u>

The Taliban who are fundamentalist Muslims led by Mullah Omar, are the remnants of the Mujahedeen and rural tribesmen who defeated the Soviet's Afghanistan invasion and took power as the government following hostilities. Taliban control of Afghanistan supposedly ended when the U.S. drove them from power during Operation Enduring Freedom as part of the Global War on Terror (GWOT) following 9/11. Taliban forces, however, continue to engage in insurgency efforts, committing violence on coalition forces and innocents in their attempts to disrupt elected governments. Taliban extremist, in Afghanistan, Iraq and, Pakistan continue to commit insurgent actions throughout the region and in attacks which they take credit for worldwide.

Currently the Taliban is engaging in expanded Information Operations (IO) to win the hearts and minds of the Afghanistan populace, by holding themselves up to be gentler

---

[12] 107TH Congress, 2D Sessions, S. Rept. NO. 107- 351 H. Rept. NO. 107-792, page 6, *Report of The Joint Inquiry Into The Terrorist Attacks Of September 11, 2001 – By The House Permanent Select Committee On Intelligence And The Senate Select Committee On Intelligence. Washington D.C.:* December 2002. (accessed at http://www.gpoaccess.gov/serialset/creports/pdf/fullreport_errata.pdf on January 6, 2010).

and kinder than in the past.[13] The Taliban's purpose in presenting themselves as kindred to the populace is a means to increase their ability to identify culturally and spiritually with the struggles and grievances of the local tribesmen. Cultural identity and common grievances resulting in commiseration make perfect tools to recruit more individuals to the extremist cause in confronting the invasion of so-called Western ‒demagoguery." An understanding of the Taliban's motivation aids in successfully combating their violent actions toward the U.S.

Understanding the Enemy, Why Is The U.S. Being Targeted?

Why is the U.S. the target of extremist Muslims? Western democratic lifestyles are an affront to true Muslim idealists who are awaiting the return of the one-world caliphate based on Salafi Jihadism. The extremist violent application of Salafi Jihadism is a fundamentalist Muslim practice derived from Sunni Islamic ideology[14]. The Salafi (an Arabic word meaning: return to the forefathers)[15] is the underlying premise for extremist opposition to Western democracies. Western freedoms, such as equality of women and the secular behaviors of the West are offensive to the pious lifestyle demanded by true Islam and are to be eradicated by the truly faithful. Fundamental Islam cannot tolerate the existence of any other than the one true God and the true Muslim lifestyle; this is the violent Jihadist philosophy pontificated by Al-Qaeda and the Taliban. A jihad or holy war is the only manner to rid the world of the infidel west. The broad

---

[13] USATODAY.com, Jim Michaels, News /World Taliban tries kinder, gentler tactics in Marjah, (accessed at http://www.usatoday.com/news/world/2010-02-22-taliban_N htm on March 20, 2010).

[14] Patrick M. Cronin-ed. *Global Strategic Assessment 2009: America's Security Role in a Changing World*, Published for the Institute for National Strategic Studies by the National Defense University Press. (Washington, D.C.: 2009). 120.

[15] Ibid. 120.

locations, extensive funding lines, and actions of over 100 terrorist groups act in support of the repudiation of modernization and promote the global *aculturalization* of Islam and the Muslim religion. The Jihadists' foundational belief is that all true Muslims have an obligation to engage in violent acts with the aim of relieving the world of corrupt values and social demagoguery. Extremist Muslims astonishingly do not see themselves as terrorists. Ramy Zamzam, one of five U.S citizens arrested in Pakistan in December 2009 on terrorism charges, stated at his court appearance, that: ―We are not terrorists, We are jihadists, and jihad is not terrorism."*[16]* One extremist's holy war is another man's terrorism, which is especially shocking when that terrorism comes from within U.S. borders.

Domestic Terrorism

Domestically, the ability of the U.S. Government to predict, identify, prevent, respond to and recover from events such as the 9/11 attacks or the attempted terrorist attacks that have occurred since 9/11 requires action from all elements of national power partnered with international allies and non-governmental stakeholders of the community of interest. Figure 1, the chart taken from the AP News and Information Research Center, Newsday article ―*List of foiled terror plots,"* delineates twenty such foiled terrorism plots[17]. The voracity and inventiveness of terrorists to exploit systemic

---

[16] Boston.com, Pamela Constable. Washington Post accessed from internet Boston Globe website, Boston.com/ *5 US ,jihadists"say they weren't planning attacks.* Http://www.boston.com/news/world/ asia/articles/2010/01/05/5_us_jihadists_say_they_werent_planning_attacks/ (accessed January 5, 2010).

[17] Associated Press News and Information Research Center, "*List of Foiled Terror Plots,"* *Newsday,* June 2, 2007, at *www.newsday.com/news/local/newyork/am-foiledplots0603 ,0,7211531.story?coll=ny-main-breakingnewslinks* ,October 19, 2007. Accessed through The Heritage

problems continues to evolve. For example: on December 25, 2009 a young Nigerian student who openly displayed militant idealist behavior and whose extremist propensity was reported to the DoS as a possible terrorist actor almost succeeded in an attempt to explode a bomb aboard an overseas flight arriving in Detroit. President Obama's statement following investigation of the incident concluded that ―inherent systemic weaknesses and human errors" were causal to the continued failure of aerial security to exploitation by terrorist.[18] President Obama then directed immediate corrective actions to provide robust standards, practices, and business processes. Too little, too late again perhaps, but this example is yet another call for comprehensive NS reform to occur.

The collaborative effort to manage the various HS roles, capabilities, equities, and jurisdictions is a daunting challenge. Operations, intelligence, and logistics require synchronization, policy staffs, and joint task forces; operating teams require integration and campaigns require coordination and unified leadership. C2 structures under reform necessitate a unity of effort operating under a unified command system to overcome an enemy bent on destruction and one that can attack from any direction. All hazards preparation and response entail every part of the community of interest's efforts.

Foundation website , article by <u>James Jay Carafano, Ph.D.</u> *U.S. Thwarts 19 Terrorist Attacks Against America Since 9/11,* November 13 2007. http://www heritage.org/Research/HomelandDefense /bg2085.cfm (accessed December 5, 2009).

[18] Barack H. Obama. "Memorandum on the Attempted Terrorist Attack on December 25, 2009: Intelligence, Screening, and Watch listing System Corrective Actions." *Daily Compilation of Presidential Documents.* (Washington,D.C.: 2010). *Academic Search Premier*, EBSCO*host* (accessed March 27, 2010). 1-3.

Increase in Number and Diversity of Terrorist Plots Against the United States Since 9/11

	2001	2002	2003	2004	2005	2006	2007	2008	2009	2010
Homegrown Violent Extremist (HVE)				4	5	6 7 8 9	11		13 14 15 16 17	21 22 23 24
al-Qa'ida	1 2		3			10			18	
Unaffiliated							12		19 20	25 26
al-Qa'ida Affiliates										27
Total Number of Plots	❷	⓿	❶	❶	❶	❺	❷	⓿	❽	❼

Target Type	Count
Civilian Other	11 Plots
Aviation	7 Plots
Military	7 Plots
Government	3 Plots
Mass Transit	3 Plots
Infrastructure	2 Plots
Financial	1 Plot

Number	Plotter or Plot Name	Targets	Number	Plotter or Plot Name	Targets
1	9/11	Civilian, Government, Aviation	13	Daniel Boyd Quantico Plot	Military
2	Richard Reid	Aviation	14	Newburgh 4	Civilian, Military, Aviation
3	Iyman Faris	Infrastructure	15	Carlos Bledsoe Little Rock Shooting	Military
4	Herald Square Plot	Mass Transit	16	Ft. Hood Shooting	Military
5	Jam'iyyat Ul-Islam Is Saheeh (JIS)	Civilian	17	Michael Finton	Government
6	Derrick Shareef	Civilian	18	Najibullah Zazi NYC Subway Plot	Mass Transit
7	Liberty 7/Sears Tower Plot	Civilian	19	Hosam Smadi	Civilian
8	Mohamed Reza Taheri Azar SUV Attack	Civilian	20	NW Flight 253	Aviation
9	Ehsanul Sadequee	Civilian, Government, Financial	21	Mohamed Osman Mohamud	Civilian
10	US-UK Aviation Plot	Aviation	22	Farooque Ahmed	Mass Transit
11	Fort Dix Plot	Military	23	Antonio Martinez	Military
12	JFK Airport Plot	Aviation	24	Paul Rockwood	Civilian
			25	Khalid Aldawsari	Military, Infrastructure
			26	Package Bomb Plot	Aviation
			27	Faisal Shahzad Times Square Plot	Civilian

This information derived from the following sources: 'American Jihadist Terrorism: Combating a Complex Threat,' Congressional Research Service, 7 December 2010; 'Al-Qaeda and Affiliates: Historical Perspective, Global Presence, and Implications for U.S. Policy' Congressional Research Service, 25 January 2011; and various criminal proceedings and Department of Justice press releases.

Figure 1: Thwarted Terrorists Plots[19]

[19]*www.fbi.govt*

Brutal violence and death are the intent of those in opposition to Western democracy and in pursuit of the return of the caliphate. Nation-state and non-state actors hate, hunt, and threaten the U.S. Government as demonstrated in the following statement by extremist leader Ayman al-Zawahiri: "The need to inflict the maximum casualties against the opponent, for this is the language understood by the West, no matter how much time and effort such operations take."[1] The most prescient evolving threat to the U.S. homeland is mujahid (mujahidin in its singular form), the literal translation of which means _ONE_ who engages in jihad.[2] Singular actors at work in concert or proximity bring terrorism to an entirely new level and require a coordinated response.

Violent, single–issue anarchists or self-styled militia groups representing everything from the national separatist movements to pro-choice, pro-life or health-care reform opposition proliferate within the borders of the U.S. and are a direct threat to U.S. populations. For OCONUS threats the "whole of government" process for effective protection of the homeland includes diplomatic, information, military, economic, financial, intelligence and law enforcement (DIMEFIL) elements, incorporating soft, hard and smart power operations. Within that process; the Department of State (DoS) utilizes diplomacy and aid packages; Office of the Director of National Intelligence (ODNI) employs information and intelligence as tools and commodities; DoD delivers kinetic actions, security and civil support assistance; and lastly, through United Nations

---

[1] Laura Mansfield. *His Own Words: Translation and Analysis of the Writings of Dr. Ayman Al Zawahiri.*, (Old Tappan, NJ:TLG Publications, 2006). 223.

[2] *Britannica Concise Encyclopedia.* s.v. "mujahidin." (accessed January 7 2010 from http://encyclopedia2.thefreedictionary.com/mujahidin).

processes and Department of Commerce actions economic sanctions are established, commerce and trade regulations to complete the holistic package of national elements of power that can be brought to bear. Attacking a new threat in a new manner includes the use of smart technology and applicability of law to identify critical vulnerabilities and remove the enemy's supporting infrastructure.

—Domestic," as a term, seemingly limits the issue to what occurs within U.S. borders, but clearly, issues such as point of origin, citizenship, governmental grievances, and religious ideologies blur the lines of what is domestic or international terrorism. Examples such as U.S. citizens who train in Al Qaeda or Taliban camps, U.S. Muslim mosques that give aid to terrorist groups or religious converts that perform violent acts in support of non-state actors demonstrate the point of blurring lines of domestic and international. Domestically the U.S. Government has advocated a —whole of government" response capability to assess, plan and respond to viable threats against the United States. Several U.S. Government agencies have equities and jurisdictions in domestic incident prevention and response also; several agencies can be inferred to have the same authorized mission and authority to direct those efforts. The problem now becomes whose job is it to direct the —whole of government" response. If the White House does not have time to manage this problem, perhaps delegation to an executive level agency is appropriate.

The Problem

The HSA of 2002 should have garnered the same unified effort for the protection of the homeland and Department of Homeland Security (DHS) as the NSA of 1947 did for the national defense and the Department of Defense (DoD).

Unity of effort would appear to be a necessary, if not mandated requirement, to ensure the security of the nation. The complexity of the threat and the nature of our adversaries coupled with the varying jurisdictions of responding bureaucracies require a clear delineation of responsibilities. DoD realizes that it does not hold the complete solution to protect the homeland as stated in the 2008 NDS:

> National security and domestic resources may be at risk, and the Department must help respond to protect lives and national assets. The Department will continue to be both bulwark and active protector in these areas. Yet, in the long run the Department of Defense is neither the best source of resources and capabilities nor the appropriate authority to shoulder these tasks. The comparative advantage, and applicable authorities, for action reside elsewhere in the U.S. Government, at other levels of government, in the private sector, and with partner nations. DoD should expect and plan to play a key supporting role in an interagency effort to combat these threats, and to help develop new capacities and capabilities, while protecting its own vulnerabilities.[3]

However, it appears from the selected passage that DoD also realizes that as the most robust element of national power, it must maintain what amounts to redundancy of mission sets like civil assistance and disaster response. The *2009 U.S. Government Counter-Insurgency (COIN) Guide*[4] speaks to application of the ―whole-of-government‖ approach to triumph over insurgency specific to Afghanistan and Pakistan issues, but DoD must remain vigilant as part of the ―whole-of-government in its supporting role domestically as well, a fact confirmed in this excerpt from the NDS:

> While defending the homeland in depth, the Department must also maintain the capacity to support civil authorities in times of national emergency such as in the wake of catastrophic natural and man-made disasters. The Department will continue to maintain consequence

---

[3] United States. *National Defense Strategy,* Department of Defense. (Washington D.C.: 2008).7.

[4] Interagency Counterinsurgency Initiative (U.S.). U.S. Government Counterinsurgency Guide. United States Government Interagency Counterinsurgency Initiative. (Washington, D.C.: 2009). 36.

management capabilities and plan for their use to support government agencies. Effective execution of such assistance, especially amid simultaneous, multi-jurisdictional disasters, requires ever-closer working relationships with other departments and agencies, and at all levels of government. To help develop and cultivate these working relationships, the Department will continue to support the Department of Homeland Security (DHS), which is responsible for coordinating the Federal response to disasters.[5]

The NS system must work together as a collective. Consequences of the US government's failure to recognize and correct systemic deficiencies in the national security system are not acceptable[6]. If it fails to provide domestic security, the U.S. Government will have to explain the preventable deaths of a mother, father, sister, brother or comrade in arms multiplied by thousands or hundreds of thousands resulting from its' failure to act. In order to mitigate the confusion in this complex environment, the Government must identify the threat, determine the nature of the threat and what government agency has lead responsibility.

Criminal or Combatant

In September 2002, law enforcement officials advised President George Bush of the existence of an alleged Al Qaeda terrorist cell, subsequently referred to as the (Lackawanna Six)[7] located in a Buffalo, New York suburb. President Bush considered the use of military units to apprehend the alleged terrorists, but decided against it. The

---

[5] United States. *National Defense Strategy*. Department of Defense, (Washington D.C.: 2008).7.

[6] The White House, Office of the Press Secretary, For Immediate Release *Remarks by the President on Security Reviews,* January 05, 2010. (Washington D.C.) (accessed at http://www. whitehouse.gov/the-press-office/remarks-president-security-reviews on January 12, 2010).

[7] United States. Statement for Immediate release, *SAHIM ALWAN SENTENCED FOR PROVIDING MATERIAL SUPPORT TO AL QAEDA*. Department of Justice, WWW.USDOJ.GOV (Washington D.C.: December 17, 2003). (accessed at http://www.fbi.gov/dojpressrel/pressrel03/ sahim121703 htm, January 10, 2010).

Lackawanna Six were eventually apprehended by the FBI, prosecuted and sentenced to between seven to ten years. The pre-arrest confusion of their status as either military combatants or criminal suspects demonstrate the blurry line between law enforcement and military operations in relation to terrorism suspects. Today's criminal justice system has adapted to a more agile investigative structure, which uses special courts to secure evidence and indictments. The use of *Foreign Intelligence Surveillance Act (FISA)* or spy courts to enable expanded investigations oscillates between evidentiary rules governing the realm of covert interventions, tribunals, and the criminal justice system. Still in contention is the question of proper prosecutorial jurisdiction. Although U.S. forces detain enemy combatants at the Guantanamo Bay Naval Base, the U.S. Supreme Court has had to provide confirmation of earlier rulings as to detainee's entitlement under the general provisions of the Geneva Convention and detainee rights under the criminal justice system, which includes the right to challenge their status as combatants or criminals.[8] The premises of the debate- whether terrorist, are soldiers or criminals; poses a complex dilemma. Professor Vardell Nesmith oftentimes espouses that: ―Men do what they do for what to them seems like good a reason at the time that they do it[9], that premise is validated in the domestic security actions of many of our past presidents. President Lincoln suspended habeas corpus to assist in prosecuting rebels and detaining suspects during the Civil War. Consequently, martial law was established to protect U.S.

---

[8] United States. *Joint Resolution to Authorize the Use of United States Armed Forces against Those Responsible for the Recent Attacks Launched against the United States*, Stat. 224. U.S. G.P.O., (Washington, D.C.:2001). 115.

[9] Dr. Vardell E. Nesmith, JR., Colonel, USA (Ret.), Professor, National Defense University, Joint Forces Staff College, (Norfolk, Va. June 2009-April 2010).

citizens and the Nation. In 1942, Franklin D. Roosevelt acted decisively to protect

America following Pearl Harbor by interning Japanese Americans and Japanese persons

residing in America without due process for crimes, which they were ―likely" to commit.

Two years later, the Supreme Court validated FDR's actions as constitutional, 44 years

later President Reagan and Congress apologized and made reparations for those same

internments. Oddly enough current immigration law uses the same basis for denial of

entry or deportation of certain persons in regards to acts of terrorism. The *Immigration

and Naturalization Act (INA) 8 United States Code (U.S.C.) 1182, section 212(a)(3)(B)(i)*

determines as inadmissible and ineligible for visas, aliens who have engaged in or are

likely to engage in terrorist activity. Many would support the acts of FDR to protect

America, as visionary and pre-emptive based on the prescience of the INA in today's

society.

An incident in the support of trial by military tribunal of legal or illegal non-

combatants is the case precedent of *Ex Parte Quirin, 317 U.S.1 (1942).*[10] This is the

1942 case of eight German saboteurs who were naturalized or had lived in the U.S.,

returned to Germany during the war, and later trained and re-entered the U.S. covertly to

destroy U.S. industry and war making capabilities. The eight were apprehended by the

FBI and fought trial by military tribunal; because they believed they were entitled to the

rights of due process in the criminal justice system. The Supreme Court upheld the

President's authority to try the saboteurs by military tribunal, not-withstanding

citizenship, or military affiliation, confirming that sovereign authority. The constitution

---

[10] US Supreme Court Center, *EX PARTE QUIRIN, 317 U. S. 1 (1942)* per curiam opinion filed
July 31, 1942, US Supreme Court Cases & Opinions, Volume 317, U. S. 22 (accessed through
Justia.com beta website http://supreme.justia.com/us/317/1/case html ,on December 2009). 317.

was visionary in providing the right of due process and protections guaranteed by and from the government but the Geneva Convention could not foresee the level of violence wielded by non-state actors in modern times. Acts committed against the U.S. by terrorists dictate the President's discretion to administer justice however he deems applicable.[11] Each application of law has its own viability, but under the Laws of Armed Conflict (LOAC) inclusive of the Geneva Convention, implied cross-functional overlap exists between military law, international treaty and the criminal justice system.

The debate which now consumes America should not be, does the Commander-in-Chief have the authority to use military tribunals but instead, does he have the will and compunction to use this authority effectively? In the cases described above, history questions the right decision at the time it occurred, for each administration Lincoln through Obama, Doctor Nesmith is right! The answer lies with the person who makes the decision based on their perception of the totality of the circumstances at the time. As demonstrated, the legal battlefield resulting from implementation of HS enforcement is as fog-filled as the kinetic battlefield. The manner in which national security missions and terrorist enforcement are organized is convoluted and duplicative. Exploration of definitions in Chapter 1 provided a confusing array of perspectives of terms; the threat examination in Chapter 2 revealed an escalating violence; and the questions of not only how but who provides comprehensive protection to the homeland remains.

---

[11] George W. Bush. "Executive Order 13440--Interpretation of the Geneva Conventions Common Article 3 as Applied to a Program of Detention and Interrogation Operated by the Central Intelligence Agency." *Weekly Compilation of Presidential Documents* 43, no. 30: 1000-1002. (Washington D.C.:2007). *Academic Search Elite*, EBSCO*host* (accessed March 27, 2010).

In Chapter 3, study of the numerous agencies, jurisdictions, and equities concerned with securing the homeland to determine which has primacy will be the focus.

CHAPTER 3

COMPARATIVE ANALYSIS: ORGANIZATION, MISSION, AUTHORITY

This chapter examines USG entities principally charged with HS/HD

responsibilities and the overlap of their missions. Congress mandated many of the 9/11

Commission's[1] recommendations to improve the security posture of the U.S. The

majority of those recommendations dealt with intelligence, disaster response and counter-

terrorism duties and the creation of the National Counterterrorism Center (NCTC). NCTC

duties require continuous threat analysis, intelligence synthesis, information sharing

within the COI and most importantly, integrating the efforts of instruments of national

power to ensure unity of effort. This integration mandate implies that the NCTC is the

lead agency for management of homeland security resources and response, but as

information reveals, the NCTC is not THE lead agency. Several agencies have lawfully

directed leadership duties for protecting America. The authorities delegated to each

organization are situationally and jurisdictionally dependent. This chapter will explain

some of the duties and responsibilities of the many agencies with HS/HD duties and

attempt to determine who is in charge.

Homeland Security roots reach back to the intent of the NSA of 1947.

Organizational structures to defend America were in place prior to 9/11 attacks and

intelligence mechanism had provided information of the transnational terrorist threat and

yet the homeland was still not prepared in September of 2001. Following the attacks, the

---

[1] National Commission on Terrorist Attacks upon the United States. The 9-11 Commission
Report, U.S. G.P.O., (Washington, D.C.: 2004). 361- 428.

HSA of 2002 and the results of the 9/11 commission provided impetus for the development of robust HS/HD organizations, processes for enhanced mass transit, upgraded border security, and improved intelligence fusion. Duties within the newly formed DHS provided security enhancements such as; increased monitoring of air, marine and other forms of mass transit to detect and intercept threats by the Transportation Security Agency (TSA); enhanced border security within the newly merged Customs and Border Protection (CBP) through additional manpower, technology updates and new processes to monitor both entry and exit of persons and materials. Also added to America's defense toolkit under the oversight of the Office of the Director of National Intelligence (ODNI) were improved intelligence collection, analysis, and fusion to develop more collaborative efforts

Legislation, intelligence, enhanced screening, forewarning and robust organizational structures should equate to a secure U.S. posture. How then does a single terrorist easily defeat terrorist screening and airport security in December of 2009?[2] To determine who is responsible as the HS/HD lead agency for enforcement and integration, an examination of the organizations responsible for HS/HD is essential.

Nexus of Defense and Security to Protecting the Homeland

There are several areas of overlap within the National Security community directly related to Homeland Defense and Homeland Security responsibilities. In order to

---

[2] ABC news.com, Richard Esposito and Brian Ross. *Investigators: Northwest Bomb Plot Planned by al Qaeda in Yemen*, 2009 at /The blotter from Brian Ross website.,website article. (accessed at http://abcnews.go.com/Blotter/al-qaeda-yemen-planned-northwest-flight-253-bomb-plot/story?id=9426085 on December 26, 2009).

meet the obligations associated with the globalization of democracy, America must align

resources in a well-organized structure that matches capability and capacity with the

specific skill set needed to address each part of the threat. Mission competencies are

divided among those organizations directly performing counter-threat duties and the need

for cross-functionality and collaboration within their primary duties assures synthesis

within the many organizations performing HS/HD functions. The overlap is articulated

in Figure 2; in which the DoD perspective of the notional relationship between HD/CS

and HS missions is depicted.

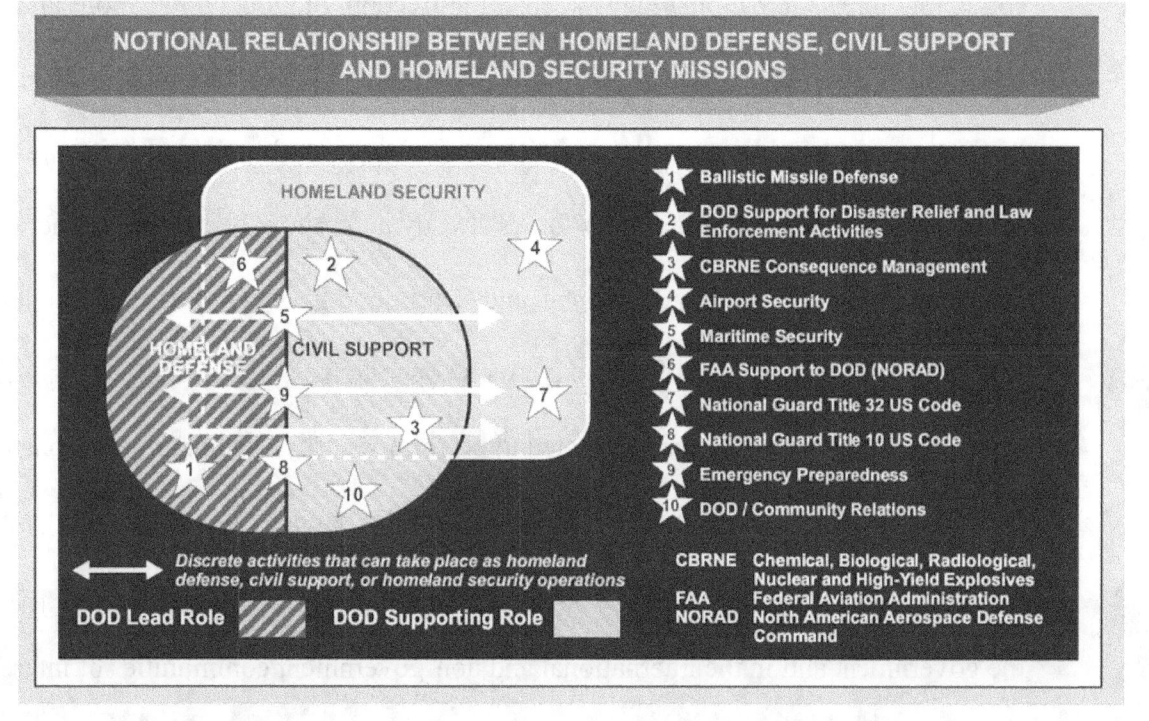

Figure 2: Notional Relationship Between Homeland Defense, Civil Support, and Homeland Security Missions[3]

---

[3] Figure taken from: United States. Joint Publication 3-28, *Civil Support*. Joint Chiefs of Staff, (Washington, D.C.: 2007). I-3.

As the figure shows, the overlap occurs when HD mission and CS missions are part of enforcement duties related to CT, incident management and recovery efforts surrounding terrorist activity. The tasks involved and the jurisdictional interests represented are too many for any one agency. DHS or DoJ would be instantly overwhelmed if tasked to investigate all crimes with a terrorism connection, while also performing humanitarian assistance and providing security and protection from further attacks. If this overlap sounds familiar, it equates back to the principles leading to the current joint-forces character of today's U.S. Armed Services. In performance of duties combating threats to national interest, ensuring freedom of global populations and modeling democracy throughout the world, the military is over-burdened. Humanitarian Assistance (HA) and Disaster Relief (DR) operations inevitably fatigue units, drawing resources and funding from military forces already unremittingly engaged in increasing kinetic operations. OEF in Afghanistan and OIF in Iraq have continued in both duration and effort well past the need for strictly kinetic operations.

Military forces are now expected to perform security, stabilization, reconstruction and rebuild functions requiring skill sets not normally requisite in military occupational specialties, until relieved. The skill sets required for such efforts exist in other areas of the government and in the international and non-government communities of interest. Building the IA capacity in parity with DoD is the missing link to facilitate the military's relief from these types of duties. Agencies such as the U.S. Agency for International Development (U.S.AID) and the U.S. Dept. of State (DoS) have the mandates to provide such services but historically have been under-resourced to supply the skill sets in the needed capacities. DoD's robust population, mission agility and "can do" responsiveness have caused U.S. reliance on their ability to solve all problems including HS/HD.

Reform in national security begins at the root effort of enabling capacity in the IA and it must be supported adequately to permit the IA the same autonomy of action previously granted to DoD forces as inferred from the following quote from President Obama on the White House Afghanistan policy,

> I'm ordering a substantial increase in our civilians on the ground. That's also why we must seek civilian support from our partners and allies, from the United Nations and international aid organizations -- an effort that Secretary Clinton will carry forward ...At a time of economic crisis, it's tempting to believe that we can shortchange this civilian effort. But make no mistake: Our efforts will fail in Afghanistan and Pakistan if we don't invest in their future. And that's why my budget includes indispensable investments in our State Department and foreign assistance programs. These investments relieve the burden on our troops. They contribute directly to security. They make the American people safer.[4]

The President's statement must be backed by action, which allow for the capacity build in IA structures to perform the duties, which follow kinetic actions. U.S. Counter-Insurgency (COIN) efforts in Iraq, Afghanistan, and Pakistan have decreased extremist presence and influence in the overseas battle-space <u>but have created an impetus for increased terrorist acts directed toward the U.S., which must be managed effectively.</u> Counter terrorism (CT) duties include the ability to identify, prevent, disrupt, or destroy terrorist networks. CT missions run the gamut from specific attacks against targets of

---

[4] The White House, Office of the Press Secretary, For Immediate Release: *Remarks by the President on a New Strategy for Afghanistan and Pakistan,* March 27, 2009. (Washington D.C.:2009). (accessed at http://www.whitehouse.gov/the_press_office/remarks-by-the-president-on-a-new-strategy-for-afghanistan-and-pakistan/ on January 12, 2010).

interests or high value targets to rendition[5] or the apprehension and surrendering of suspects to the COI for processing in keeping with applicable laws of that country.

Counter-Terrorism (CT) duties also require a strong set of mission skills and intelligence fusion across the enforcement spectrum. As CT duties relate to domestic terrorism, applicable laws and jurisdictions in responding to terrorist events on U.S. soil constrict the military. DHS, the entity responsible for both development and implementation of the National Response Framework (NRF), facilitates U.S. national preparation and response efforts for catastrophic events. Upon implementation of the NRF, resources such as personnel or equipment utilized in response efforts remain under the operational control of their organizational chains of command but the combined multi-agency command system (MACS) has tactical control (TACON) to direct their efforts. Perhaps applicability of the NRF system is an alternative paradigm for coordination of CT operations.

Terrorism has shown a correlative overlap to the criminal narcotics trade and DoD resources have a long history providing support to law enforcement Counter-Narcotics Enforcement (CNE) operations. Military commands performing missions in direct support of law enforcement CNE missions in joint task forces may have TACON over civilian agencies, such as occurs in Joint Inter-Agency Task Forces (JIATF) South and West. Counter-Narcotics Enforcement (CNE) and interdiction operations are conceived at the national level by the Office of National Drug Control Policy (ONDCP) to reduce

---

[5] Rendition refers to a tactic which involves capture of a person and transfer of that person to another location: for example a suspected terrorist might be captured in a nation with strict torture laws, that person would be transferred to another nation with more lenient torture laws in order to extract information.

the drug threat posed to the U.S. International and Inter-agency partnerships link through the ONDCP allowing federal, state, local, tribal and non-governmental agencies to support operations to reduce trafficking, diminish narco-terrorism and provide rehabilitation services. Cooperative efforts in all aspects from country of origin through treatment for addiction demonstrate the need for and efficacy of holistic approaches to accomplish threat declination. The connection between crime and terrorism dictate coordinated enforcement responses similar to joint combat operations. Collaborative efforts such as JIATF-South validate the proven effectiveness of cooperative response to the narcotics threat. The ―whole of government" approach at work in SOUTHCOM's JIATF-South is indicative of the synergistic efforts in operations and intelligence fusion required to manage the threat of narcotics proliferation.

Intelligence collection and analysis structures capable of providing products and networks to avoid strategic surprise assist in directing kinetic operations and improving real time targeting. To be effective these structures must organize to provide maximum synthesis in the Intelligence Community (IC). The Office of the Director of National Intelligence (ODNI), created in 2005, is structured to coordinate and integrate the intelligence efforts of the IC. The membership of the IC includes: representation from each armed service, the Coast Guard (U.S.CG), Central Intelligence Agency (CIA), Defense Intelligence Agency (DIA), Department of Energy (DOE), Department of Homeland Security (DHS), Department of State (DoS), Department of Treasury (DoT), Drug Enforcement Administration (DEA), Federal Bureau of Investigation (FBI), National Geospatial –Intelligence Agency (NGIA), National Reconnaissance Office (NRO), and the National Security Agency Central Security Service ((NSA/CSS).

Synthesis, fusion, and coordination of intelligence is essential to comprehensive NS and at some point it must be combined with operational coordination. During the cooperative coalition efforts, which occur currently, the processes of entities from international organizations, nation states, IGOs and NGOs integrate to provide kinetic actions or stabilization and reconstruction efforts. An overall view of the comparative organizational structures of international, national, military, federal, state, local and non-governmental agencies is demonstrated in Figure 3.

The generosity and benevolence of the U.S. are never more clearly demonstrated than when participating in operations that protect non-combatants, foster security, and stability or provide assistance and recovery following catastrophic events. Humanitarian Assistance (HA) and Disaster Recovery (DR) situations lend themselves to an OCONUS paradigm however; emergency response and preparedness duties include several U.S. Government and NGOs ideally structured for domestic and international missions. Internationally, under assistance to NATO or the United Nations, the U.S. Government may deploy DoD, DoS or DHS resources as part of a combined global response within the parameters provided in law and treaties. Domestically, DHS's mandate is development, implementation, and monitoring of the National Response Framework (NRF) in effectively managing federal, state, local government and non-government agency response to domestic incidents. There is a significant inference drawn from the similarity in skill sets required to provide domestic HA/DR and those required for OCONUS stability, rebuild and reconstruction efforts. An investment, which builds significant capacity into domestic response, through hiring and training practices, will result in an increased level of expertise and capacity available for OCONUS response.

COMPARISON OF AGENCY ORGANIZATIONAL STRUCTURES

| | ARMED FORCES OF THE UNITED STATES | EXECUTIVE DEPARTMENTS & AGENCIES | STATE & LOCAL GOVERNMENT | REGIONAL AND INTERNATIONAL | | NGOs AND PVOs |
				NORTH ATLANTIC TREATY ORGANIZATION (NATO)	UNITED NATIONS (UN)	
STRATEGIC	Secretary of Defense Chairman of the Joint Chiefs of Staff Joint Chiefs of Staff Combatant Commander (1)	National Headquarters Department Secretaries	Governor	NATO Headquarters Supreme Allied Commander, Europe (SACEUR)	UN Headquarters Functional Headquarters (e.g. UN High Commissioner for Refugees)	National Headquarters
OPERATIONAL	Combatant Commander Combatant Commander, Joint Task Force (CJTF) (2) Defense Coordinating Officer/Defense Coordinating Element	Ambassador/Embassy (3) Liaisons (4) Federal Coordinating Officer (FCO) Regional Office	State Adjutant General State Coordinating Officer (SCO) Office of Emergency Services (OES) Department/Agency	Major Subordinate Commands (e.g. Allied Forces Southern Europe)	Special Representative to the Secretary General (6) UN Command Korea, when activated, is the only UN organization at the operational level.	(Some organizations have regional offices)
TACTICAL	CJTF Components Service Functional	Ambassador/Embassy Field Office US Agency for International Development/Office of US Foreign Disaster Assistance Disaster Response Team Liaison (5) Response Team	National Guard County Commissioner Mayor/Manager County City (e.g. Police Department)	Principal Subordinate Commands (e.g. Allied Land Forces Southern Europe) Commander, Combined Joint Task Force Task Element Task Unit	Special Representative to the Secretary General Military Force Commander Teams Observers	Field Office In Program Country Relief Workers

1. The combatant commander, within the context of unified action, may function at both the strategic and operational levels in synchronizing the application of all instruments of national power in time, space, and purpose with the actions of other military forces, USG agencies, NGOs and PVOs, regional and international organizations, and corporations toward theater strategic objectives.
2. The commander, joint task force (CJTF), within the context of unified action, functions at both the operational and tactical levels in synchronizing the application of all instruments of national power in time, space, and purpose with the actions of other military forces, USG agencies, NGOs and PVOs, regional and international organizations, and corporations toward theater operational objectives.
3. The Ambassador and Embassy (which includes the country team) function at both the operational and tactical levels by supporting joint operation planning conducted by a combatant commander or CJTF.
4. Liaisons at the operational level may include the Foreign Policy Advisor (FPA) or Political Advisor (POLAD) assigned to the combatant commander by the Department of State, the CIA liaison officer, or any specifically assigned person. Other USG agencies do not have a similar counterpart to the combatant commander.
5. USAID's Office of US Foreign Disaster Assistance (OFDA) provides its rapidly deployable Disaster Assistance Response Team (DART) in response to international disasters. A DART provides specialists, trained in a variety of disaster relief skills, to assist US embassies and USAID missions with the management of US Government response to disasters.
6. The Special Representative to the UN Secretary General may function at both the operational and tactical levels.

Figure 3: Comparison of Agency Organizational Structure[6]

[6] United States. Joint Publication 3-08, *Interagency, Intergovernmental Organization, and Nongovernmental Organization Coordination During Joint Operations Vol. I*. Joint Chiefs of Staff, (Washington, D.C.: 2006). I-7.

The comparison chart provides perspective from international to IA and non-government organizations (NGO) at the strategic, operational, and tactical levels. The organizational comparisons that follow in the chapter view major HD/HS entities and their similar and dissimilar functionality to demonstrate gaps, seams, and redundancy.

Homeland Defense NSC/DoD Model
National Security Council (NSC)

The NSA of 1947 codified and further developed the IA process begun in World War II to manage the redundant authorities present within the War Department and executive cabinet at the time. The National Security Council (NSC) was created from the NSA of 1947 as a means to proliferate a national strategic direction for collective U.S. Government defense efforts. The primary duty of the NSC is to advise the President with regard to policy on foreign and domestic national security issues. The NSC consists of four statutorily authorized permanent members, the President, Vice President and the Secretaries of State and Defense, other non-statutory but permanent members are the National Security Advisor, Secretary of the Treasury, Director of National Intelligence (DNI), Chairman of the Joint Chiefs of Staff (CJCS) other department and agency directors designated by the President or as necessitated by the situation. The staff of the NSC is approximately 240 personnel working under the direct authority of the Executive Office of the President (EOP) and managed by the Assistant to the President for National Security Affairs or as otherwise known the National Security Adviser. The NSC over the years has developed and evolved manifesting itself to reflect the aims and priorities of each president. NSC influence on policy has ebbed and flowed based on the personalities of each administration, but not without its own problems.[7]

Until September 11, 2001, the NSC was the principle coordination entity for those agencies (mainly DoD, DoS and the CIA) responsible for protecting America. The majority of national security work performed by these agencies was OCONUS. No one gave credence to significant radical violence occurring on U.S. soil; there were other NSC priorities. Information revealed in the 9/11-Commission report inferred that "lip service" was given to the NSC staff and its advisory duties were not primary focus:

> Even as it crowds into every square inch of available office space, the NSC staff is still not sized or funded to be an executive agency….Yet a subtle and more serious danger is that as the NSC staff is consumed by these day-to-day tasks, it has less capacity to find the time and detachment needed to advise a president on larger policy issues.[8]

In February 2001, under National Security Presidential Directive-1(NSPD-1), the NSC reorganized to a more streamlined organization with more functional capabilities and has since garnered a role with greater emphasis. The NSC process currently includes meetings of the NSC Principals Committee (NSCPC formalized in the Clinton administration) in which interagency Cabinet-level officials examine national issues that do not require the President's input. The NSC Deputies Committee (NSCDC) consisting of the deputies of the Principals Committee examine U.S. policy issues affecting national security as well as developing and monitoring the interagency implementation process.

---

[7] D. Robert Worley. *The National Security Council: Recommendations for the New President.* IBM Center for the Business of Government, (Washington D.C.:2009).

[8] National Commission on Terrorist Attacks upon the United States. *The 9/11 Commission Report: Final Report of the National Commission on Terrorist Attacks Upon the United States,* (Norton, New York: 2004). 402

Prior to the Bush administration, the implementation of Presidential policy decisions were the duties of various Interagency Working Groups (IWGs). Under President Bush the IWG process was abolished and replaced with NSC Policy Coordination Committees (NSC/PCCs). The current process for managing implementation of national security policies as directed by Presidential Policy Directive-1 (PPD-1) and White Hose memorandums accomplishes the tasks via Interagency Policy Committees (IPC)[9] organized geographically by designated regions and functionally by issues. Policy issues requiring further study and monitored implementation are delegated to sub-IPCs or sub-interagency policy coordination groups for disposition. The NSC structure and relationships are depicted in Figure 4: *National Security Council Organization*.

Clearly, the President with responsibilities to safeguard the national security interest of America imbues the NSC with authority and direction. The common perception is that the NSC and DoD concentrate on OCONUS defense and security efforts and that the HSC and DHS along with the domestic COI focus their efforts domestically. The separation as functionally described leaves gaps, creates seams and provides the opportunity for exploitation. The environment of national security, homeland security, and homeland defense is comprehensive and fraught with overlapping equities of the functional focus of each agency. The global commons depend on the

---

[9] Barack H. Obama. *Organization of the National Security Council System*. Presidential Policy Directive-1. PPD-1, (Washington, D.C.: 2009). Each administration establishes the structure and processes for the NSC per Presidential preference. PPD-1also rescinded NSPD-8.

holistic approach for mutually assured protection; without it the U.S. and the community

of interest can only be certain of mutually assured destruction.

NATIONAL SECURITY COUNCIL ORGANIZATION				
	Office of the Secretary of Defense	Joint Staff	Department of State	Other Executive Branch
NATIONAL SECURITY COUNCIL	Secretary of Defense	Chairman of the Joint Chiefs of Staff	Secretary of State	President, Vice President, Secretary of the Treasury, Assistant to the President for National Security Affairs, Director of Central Intelligence, Chief of Staff to the President, Assistant to the President for Economic Policy, Attorney General, Director OMB, Counsel to the President
PRINCIPALS COMMITTEE	Secretary of Defense	Chairman of the Joint Chiefs of Staff	Secretary of State	Secretary of the Treasury, Director of Central Intelligence, Chief of Staff to the President, Attorney General, Director OMB, Counsel to the President, Chief of Staff to the Vice President, Assistant to the President and Deputy National Security Advisor, et al.
DEPUTIES COMMITTEE	Deputy Secretary of Defense or Undersecretary for Policy	Vice Chairman of the Joint Chiefs of Staff	Deputy Secretary of State	Assistant to the President for National Security Affairs and other deputies of Principals
POLICY COORDINATION COMMITTEES (PCCs)				
PCCs - Regional	Europe and Eurasia East Asia Near East and North Africa		Western Hemisphere South Asia Africa	
PCCs - Functional	Democracy, Human Rights, and International Operations International Development and Humanitarian Assistance Global Environment International Finance Transnational Economic Issues Counterterrorism and National Preparedness Defense Strategy, Force Structure, and Planning Arms Control Proliferation, Counterproliferation, and Homeland Defense Intelligence and Counterintelligence Records Access and Information Security			

Figure 4: National Security Council Organization[10]

---

[10] United States. Joint Publication 3-08, *Interagency, Intergovernmental Organization, and Nongovernmental Organization Coordination During Joint Operations Vol. I*. Joint Chiefs of Staff, (Washington, D.C.: 2006). II-4.

In 2009, the Obama administration like administrations before reorganized the NSC and HSC to fit their model for functionality. The administration based its reorganization on recommendations included in the results of Presidential Study Directive -1 (PSD-1) which was a directed interagency review of White house organization for HS and CT.[11] The most significant recommendation implemented was the integration of the NSC and HSC into the National Security staff under the National Security Advisor. This merger was a momentous step towards NS reform in the last decade as it demonstrates Presidential level emphasis in removing the bureaucratic obstructions that have hindered a comprehensive solution. The actions resulting from PSD-1 and Presidential Policy Directive (PPD-1)[12] will be further discussed in chapters 5 and 6 and an example organizational structure chart is included in Appendix V.

United States Northern Command (NORTHCOM)

Established in October 2002, NORTHCOM is the lead DoD agency for Homeland Defense, Civil Support and integration of DoD efforts in support of Homeland Security. NORTHCOM is directed by the President or the SECDEF under the DoD Unified Command Plan (UCP) to –anticipate and conduct Homeland Defense missions and Civil Support (CS) operations within the assigned area of responsibility in support of the U.S. and its interests". NORTHCOM is responsible for assisting federal, state or local civil authorities in the contiguous U.S., Alaska, Puerto Rico and the U.S. Virgin Islands, and borders with Canada and Mexico as well as portions of the Caribbean. NORTHCOM's Commander has dual command responsibility as Commander of North American Aerospace Defense Command (NORAD). NORAD's bi-national duties with Canada

---

[11] Barack H. Obama. *Organizing for Homeland Security and Counterterrorism*. Presidential Study Directive-1. PSD-1.(Washington, D.C.: 2009).

[12] Barack H. Obama. *Organization of the National Security Council System*. Presidential Policy Directive-1. PPD-1. (Washington, D.C.: 2009).

include aerospace, aerial, and marine surveillance, monitoring and early warning of the North American continent. As the DoD element providing HD, NORTHCOM's duties overlap DHS responsibilities as the monitoring and patrolling of America's domestic air, land and sea borders is a shared responsibility with cross-functional jurisdictions conceptually it represents a dimensionally layered complete system. The NORTHCOM command structure contains functionally designated subordinate commands and task forces under its purview to complete its HD and CS missions, Appendix I synopsizes the NORTHCOM organizational elements. NORTHCOM's HD success depends on its ability to conduct effective supported/ supporting functions and expediency of effort derived from long-standing relationships with the interagency.

Figure 5: NORTHCOM Organization Chart[13]

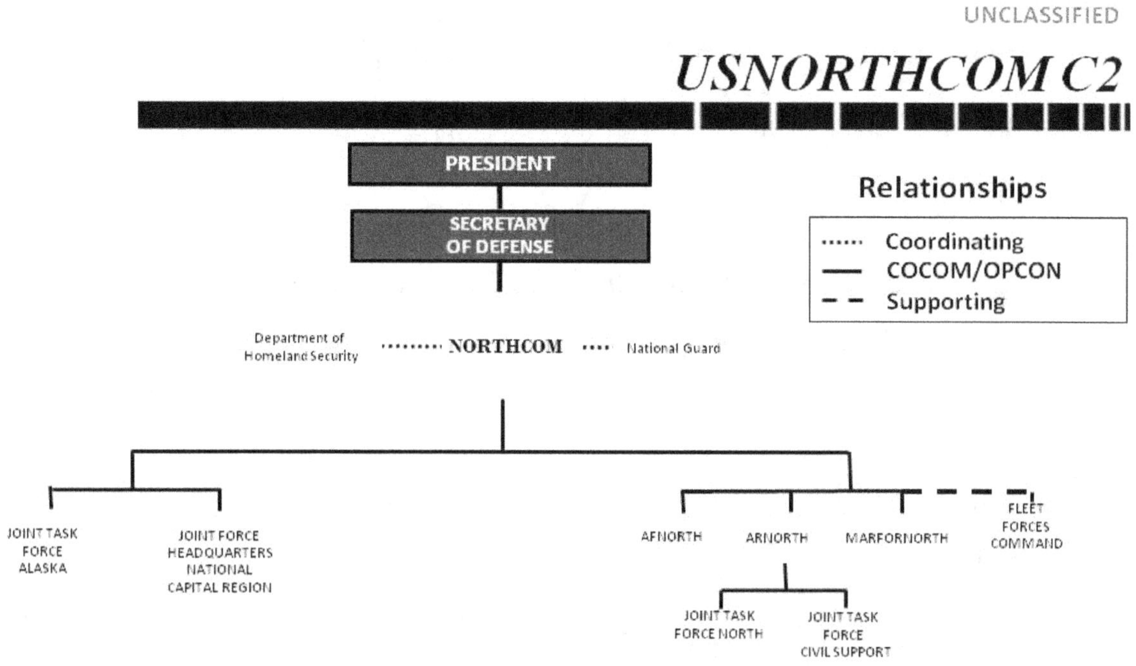

---

[13] NORTHCOM Organizational Structure, Executive Office of NORAD/NORTHCOM Chief of Staff: PowerPoint slide. Peterson AFB, CO. April 2010.

Confusion of Command Relationships

Consistent with DoD doctrine established in *Joint Publication 3-08 and JP 3-27,* in either OCONUS or domestic arenas, military resources will always be under the tactical command of military commanders.[14 and 15] During certain circumstances such as disaster relief, law enforcement or civil support missions DoD resources may fall under the administrative direction of civilians. The tactical control of the established Title 10, 32, or state active duty military chain of command remains intact using a unity of effort model. For OCONUS Homeland Defense missions, DoD assumes leadership with other federal agencies in support. For domestic incident management (DoD speak for Homeland Security missions) DoD is in a supporting role of the lead federal agency. The confusion of command and control occurs when an incident involves law enforcement, active homeland defense or terrorism elements. DoD, DHS and DoJ each have equities, responsibilities and jurisdictional overlap in these types of incidents.

NSD/DoD and IA Best Efforts

NORTHCOM's functional base of capabilities coupled with collaboration demonstrates a mixture of diverse entities for a synergetic HD response. NORTHCOM Commander, General Victor E. Renuart Jr. stated the following:

> It's the collective 'we' - it's not 'me,' it's not 'you,' it's all of us... Combined planning, combined execution, integrated planning - all of that is ... where we

---

[14] United States. *Interagency, Intergovernmental Organization, and Nongovernmental Organization Coordination During Joint Operation, Joint Publication 3-08, Vol. I.* Joint Chiefs of Staff, (Washington, D.C.:2006).

[15] United States. *Homeland Defense. Joint Pub 3-27.* Joint Chiefs of Staff, (Washington, D.C.: 2007).

want to continue to go…. "We want to make sure that the integration of our efforts doesn't show a seam but rather shows seamless support.[16]

Renuart speaks to the heart of what is required for efficacy at the HD/HS execution level. Synergy evolves from bringing all the seemingly cogent partners to the table for input, not as an afterthought but from contingency planning which occurs long before phase zero begins. Without that preventive mindset and vision, the enemy exploits seams and gaps.

Lastly, General Renuart stressed the importance of why unity of effort is required from the IC in this statement: "It requires U.S. to have this community of interest - a mega-community of sorts - that allows U.S. to pull together our local, our state, our federal, military, civilian, active and Reserve component experts to be able to provide unity of effort to ensure that your families, my families are protected.[17]

2010 DoD Quadrennial Defense Review (QDR)

The DoD role in HS is normally perceived as kinetic military based actions, law enforcement type actions belong to DoJ and DHS. As discussed in prior chapters DoD duties are no longer limited to kinetic combat operations. New mission sets in support of humanitarian assistance, nation-building, peacekeeping and reconstruction are in demand overseas and domestically. The DoD QDR released February 2010 reflects its HD role in support of HS as part of the comprehensive U.S. Government COI approach: —The

---

[16] Army.Mil website article: Staff Sgt. Jim Greenhill, *Guard, NORTHCOM partner to defend homeland, March 04 2009. Remarks of Air Force Gen. Gene Renuart, Commander of North American Aerospace Defense Command and U.S. Northern Command, tells attendees at the National Guard's 2009 Domestic Operations Workshop.* http://www.army.mil/-news/2009/03/04/17760-guard-northcom-partner-to-defend-homeland/.

[17] Ibid, Army.Mil website article

Department of Defense supports the Department of Homeland Security, and other federal civilian agencies, as part of a whole-of-government, whole-of-nation approach to both domestic security and domestic incident response."[18]

HOMELAND SECURITY HSC/DHS MODEL

Homeland Security Council (HSC)

The Homeland Security Council (HSC) established by Executive Order 13228 of October 8, 2001 is the U.S. government, inter-agency body that provides advice to the President specific to homeland security issues and peripherally on other national security policy issues. HSC is organized per Homeland Security Presidential Directive-1 (HSPD-1) incorporating both HSC Principals and Deputies Committees with Policy Coordination Committees (PCC) used for analysis of prescient national security issues and implementation of HS policy. HSC almost duplicates the NSC structure and processes except with primary focus on domestic security policy and the requirement to protect U.S. from nation and non-nation actors through domestic incident management of catastrophic events.

The HSC's focus is primarily domestic security interests. Though the functional overlap of the two security committees seems plain to discern, HSC's intersection with NSC focus is problematic in the objectives, authorities, jurisdictions, and operational provision of the security/defense function. Both the HSC and the NSC share many of the same threat concerns and perform duplicative functions to complete their respective missions.

---

[18] Robert M. Gates. *Quadrennial Defense Review Report,* Dept. of Defense. (Washington, D.C.: 2010). 70.

Preparation, training, and evaluation of processes requires a continual evaluation mechanism to remain valid. The HSC, DHS and the HS COI, developed 15 National Planning scenarios, which are used to develop and evaluate National Contingency Plans (CONPLAN) and Crisis Action Plans (CAP) as annexes that address each scenario under the National Exercise Program (NEP). The NEP incorporates National Level Exercises (NLE) and Principal Level Exercises (PLE) to promote interagency strategic planning and coordination under a five-tier exercise program addressing participation by executive and cabinet level personnel, federal agencies, non-federal agencies and non-government organizations participation. Contingency Operations and Crisis Action Plans are further evaluated under the Homeland Security Exercise and Evaluation Program (HSEEP). Tabletop and practical exercises derived from each plan then test the National Response Framework (NRF) and Incident Command System (ICS) for interoperability and proficiency under simulated crisis conditions. Figure 6 illustrates the planning relationships, which generate the agency efforts from application of national strategic guidance through implementation of local tactical plans. The similarity of infrastructure and lines of communication involved in incident management are available for use within a coordinated structure for day-today National Security System management.

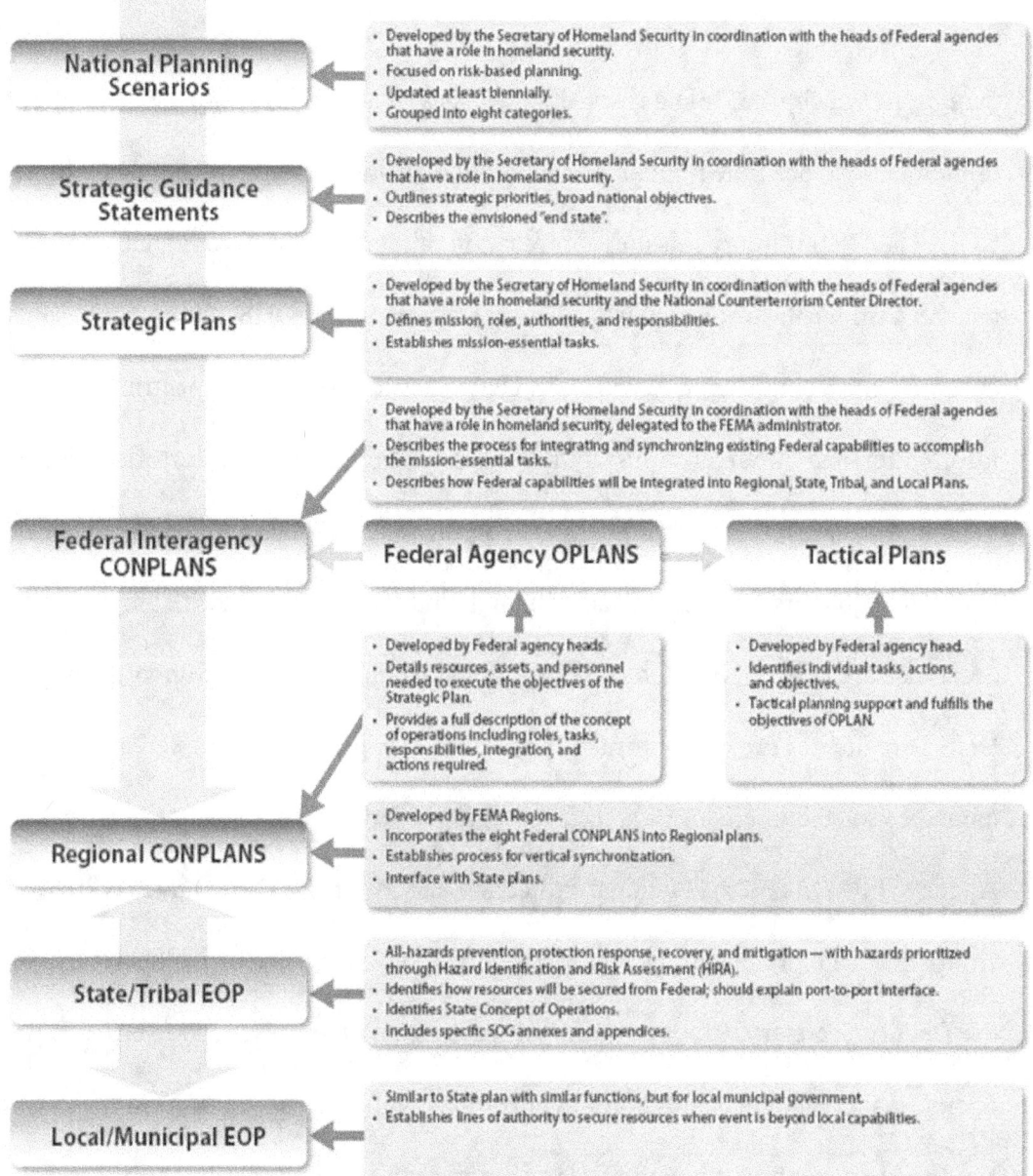

Figure 6: Federal and State Planning Relationships[19]

Department of Homeland Security (DHS)

President George Bush signed the Homeland Security Act (HSA) into law in

November of 2002, directing the establishment of DHS. DHS's organizational stand-up

on March 1, 2003 was in the wake of 9/11 causing a shift in the national security

[19] United States. *Developing and Maintaining State, Territorial, Tribal, and Local Government Emergency Plans*. Dept. of Homeland Security, FEMA (Washington, D.C.: 2009). 4-10.

paradigm. Much like DoD's rise from the ashes of WWII, the purpose of DHS is to implement and promote joint and collaborative efforts between the entities within the HS COI. The DHS primary mission is protection of the homeland from attack and HS recovery from catastrophic events. The transformation of DHS combined 22 separate agencies into a single agency with responsibilities across the full spectrum of HS, information and intelligence fusion, immigration, border security, terrorism, international trade and commerce, and emergency preparedness and response. DHS is organized into DHS Headquarters staff functions, (which includes all DHS support components, unless otherwise specified); Directorates, Operational Components, and Support Components. DHS Directorates are components (operational or support) that were created and so named by statute; includes organizations such as Federal Emergency Management Agency (FEMA) and the National Protection and Programs Directorate (NPPD). DHS components are organizations that report directly to the Office of the Secretary, such as the Deputy Secretary, Chief of Staff, Counselors, and their respective staffs. DHS operational components are those organizations with specific centralized responsibility for directly achieving a specific DHS mission, such as: the US Coast Guard's (USCG) maritime protection duties or Customs and Border Protection's (CBP) air, land, and marine border inspection duties. DHS support components generally provide specific assistance and/or guidance to other DHS components and/or external organizations within the HS COI.

DHS is the face of U.S. Homeland Security, encompassing agencies with missions regulating cross-border trade and commerce, air, land and sea border security, transportation screening, cargo inspection, citizenship and immigration services and customs enforcement. The diversity of DHS missions often dictates that their law enforcement components are cross-trained and cross-designated in different disciplines. As regards U.S. disaster preparedness and emergency response, DHS is statutorily designated to lead prevention, contingency and crisis planning, response, recovery, and resilience efforts of not only the U.S. government but also the nation as a whole for catastrophic events. Catastrophic events encompass the totality of incidents either nature based or human derived. State and local jurisdictions depend on the U.S. government in times of dire need and DHS is the federal representative for coordinating that response. DHS must facilitate national interoperability and preparedness through implementation of cooperative and collaborative constructs such as the National Incident Management System (NIMS), the Incident Command System (ICS) and the Integrated Planning System (IPS) across federal, state, local, tribal and non-government organizations. These collective and "infinite" mission sets fall into the DHS purview but are consistent with missions carried out by other federal, state, and local organizations. The DHS structure is too complex to elaborate on the numerous individual components, Figure 7 depicts the DHS organizational structure and Appendix II will briefly describes the DHS Operational Centers with significant HS duties specifically related to counter-terrorism culminating with the DHS National Operations Center.

The DHS NOC's strategic mission is to function as a national fusion cell that synthesizes information from other operations centers to provide national situational awareness, communications and operations coordination, dispensing real-time intelligence to the President, federal, state, and local law enforcement agencies.

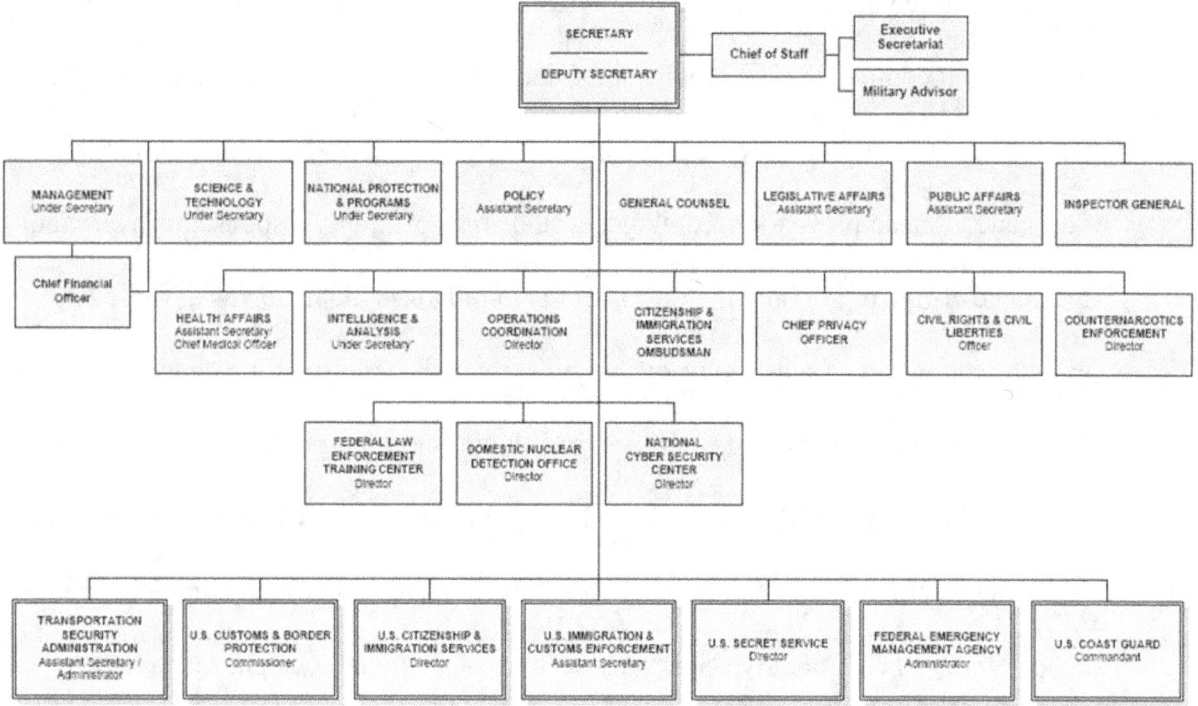

Figure 7: DHS Organizational Chart[20]

The NOC coordinates with the White House situation room and multiple IA operation centers from DoD, DoJ, NGOs and other LE functions to provide a unity of effort for the prevention of terrorist attacks and domestic incident management. Some 35 Federal, State, territorial, tribal, local, and private sector agencies collect and fuse information within the NOC. Divided into law enforcement operations and intelligence functions the NOC synthesizes intelligence into operational counter-terrorist actions by law enforcement personnel. It is a proactive, collaborative effort, which is effective as a unity of effort model, not based on command and control.

---

[20] DHS Website, Organizational chart. http://www.dhs.gov/xlibrary/assets/DHS_OrgChart.pdf (accessed on March 28,2010).

2010 Quadrennial Homeland Security Review (QHSR)

The 2010 QHSR introduces the HS ‑enterprise" lexicon in keeping with the DHS approach of conducting business; it promotes unity of effort, vice command and control structures. The rapidity and volatility with which the threats to America change, and the uncertainty of known variables comprising that threat require communal if not global solutions. Gaps and seams within the HS dilemma are both complex and ambiguous simultaneously. The definition in the current QHSR takes into account the ever-changing threat picture, the overlapping jurisdictional conflicts and the lack of clarity in coordinating the agencies roles and responsibilities. Framing the commonality of the problem, the threat, the definitions and, the roles and mission, allows for synergetic response.

HS is the one enterprise that we must all undertake or risk perishing from failure to act in concert. The ‑HS Enterprise" is not just nationally but globally reflected in our duty to each other. A quote from famous critic and poet G.K. Chesterton so aptly describes the HS environment, the threat and the solution: "We are all in the same boat on a stormy sea and we owe each other a terrible loyalty."[21] In application of the elements of national power and pursuit of national interests, the U.S. exhibits its cultivation of global support, peace and prosperity, therefore globally, we are our ‑brother's keeper" and that effort begins at home. The February 2010 QHSR is the result of the first congressionally mandated security review in the department's history. The QHSR represents a

---

[21] Encyclopedia Britannica Online. Gilbert Keith Chesterton "G.K. Chesterton." s.v. Encyclopedia Britannica. 2010. (accessed at http://www.britannica.com/EBchecked/topic/109780/G-K-Chesterton on 07 Mar. 2010).

comprehensive examination of homeland security to provide direction to the department for the next four years and update U.S. national security strategies, plans, and courses of action. The QHSR five mission areas based on DHS responsibilities are: preventing terrorism and enhancing domestic security, securing and managing our borders, smart and tough enforcement and administration of immigration laws, safeguarding and securing cyberspace, ensuring resilience to disasters and lastly, the agency will continue to mature and unify the diverse organizations that it has combined to become DHS.[22] The review of processes, planning efforts, response plans, departmental capabilities and resources allotments included input from the community of interest regarding transportation system security, critical infrastructure/key resource protection, cyber security, domestic WMD/CBRN protection, and protection of U.S. national interests were influential to the QHSR outcome.

The DHS Strategic Plan 2008-2013 is based on a five-year plan and subject to update based on the new HS enterprise construct; however, DHS business practices will continue per current doctrine and policy. The enterprise concept embraces the current administration's transparency of government and holistic problem-solving approach, involving the COI stakeholders in essential aspects of HS, such as emergency preparedness and catastrophic incident response.[23] DHS strategic guidance provides overall direction for the department and communicates its strategic goals and objectives.

---

[22] U.S. Government, Department of Homeland Security, Quadrennial Homeland Security Review Report. (Washington D.C.: 2010). X (accessed at http://www.dhs.gov/xlibrary/assets/ qhsr_executive_summary.pdf on February, 2010).

[23] United States. *One Team, One Mission, Securing Our Homeland U.S. Department of Homeland Security Strategic Plan, Fiscal Years 2008-2013.* The Department, (Washington, D.C.: 2008). 6-36.

The simplistic view of strategic goals in the DHS Strategic Plan are: protection of the U.S. from dangerous people, protection of the U.S. from dangerous goods, protection of critical infrastructure, strengthening U.S. preparedness and emergency response capabilities and improving DHS operations and management. Within the strategic plan, operational objectives support DHS strategic goals and are consistent with the U.S. national security vision and aims, all of which enable successful realization of achievable national interest, to maintain the global commons. Facilitation of comprehensive HS effectually results in a defense-in-depth model, originating with local plans encompassed within state plans, annexed into federal contingency plans. These elements of national response are managed through implementation of programs such as the National Response Framework (NRF), National Incident Management System, and Incident Command System, making possible increased interoperability and effective unified command structures. The reality is that DHS must actively involve other Federal IA, state, local, tribal, non-government institutions (NGO) and international partners in its efforts to identify, prevent, manage and respond to terrorist threats, major disasters. Per the DHS strategic plan: ―We will continue to work cooperatively to ensure that all of the instruments of national power (including leadership, specialized technical expertise, research, and development investments) are brought to bear on the challenges we face in a coordinated and unified manner."[24]

---

[24] United States. *One Team, One Mission, Securing Our Homeland U.S. Department of Homeland Security Strategic Plan, Fiscal Years 2008-2013,* The Department, (Washington, D.C.: 2008). 6-36.

Confusion of Statutory Lead Organization Role

Although the major entities previously stated for discussion in this chapter are NSC/DoD and HSC/DHS, the Department of Justice (DoJ), specifically the Federal Bureau of Investigation (FBI) and the Office of the Director of National Intelligence (ODNI) maintain significant resources pertinent to HS/HD duties. These agencies are discussed at this point and in this manner to illustrate the vastness of the mission, resource overlap and command confusion connected to this subject.

Department of Justice

The FBI is statutorily responsible for the investigation of terrorist acts and foreign intelligence threats directed at the U.S. This does not limit their investigative duties to the U.S. It simply connects the jurisdiction of the FBI to the U.S. role as a stakeholder in global security interests. FBI overseas investigations demonstrate the likelihood that acts of international terrorism, which are in the purview of FBI jurisdiction often, connect to domestic terrorism. The global nature of the terrorism threat must be traced back to its origin and when that threat is located, all elements of national power must be directed to prosecute or ameliorate it. The FBI has multiple resource effects available to complete its mission. The following are synopsis of FBI resources with HS related missions:

Strategic Information and Operations Center (SIOC) is the FBI's organizational unit for managing multiple crises through the collaborative efforts of 38 U.S. agencies. The SIOC serves as a central control hub for all federal intelligence, law enforcement, and investigative law enforcement activities related to domestic terrorist incidents and credible threats to U.S. interest. National situational awareness and multi-crisis management place SIOC at the center of HS operational response.

National Joint Terrorism Task Force (NJTTF) is the HQ element of the National Joint Task Force effort, made up of over 40 member agencies. The NJTTF provides direction and support of over 100 JTTFs located throughout the U.S. enabling real-time fusion and distribution of intelligence within the community of interest. Nationally, JTTFs investigate domestic terrorism leads, gather evidence, make arrests, provide security for special events, conduct training, collect and share intelligence, and provide rapid response to threats and incidents at a moment's notice. These duties place the NJTTF and JTTFs on the front line of domestic CT duties pertinent to HS.

National Security Branch (NSB). The NSB oversees the actions of the Counterterrorism Division (CTD), Counterintelligence Division (CD), Directorate of Intelligence (DI), and Weapons of Mass Destruction Directorate (WMDD), combining their missions, capabilities, and resources into a collective intra-agency tool, which includes the inherent IA resources of each. Notionally, the varieties of internal disciplines and external interactions and interoperability as well as IA jurisdictional overlap are leveraged for effective information sharing and operational collaboration within NSB.

Terrorist Screening Center (TSC). The consolidated database of identifying information of known or suspected terrorist is maintained by the TSC. LE agencies have 24-hour access to the information through the NTC or the computerized National Crime Information Center (NCIC). The information is compiled through investigation and from DoS designations acquired through visa denials and supporting information.

Terrorist Threat Integration Center (TTIC). The FBI also manages TTIC, which is responsible for integration and analysis of the daily fusillade of threats and intelligence.

The TTIC gathers collection products from the intelligence community of law enforcement, homeland security, diplomatic, and military sources. TTIC provides comprehensive analysis of threats and intelligence fusion to the same community for appropriate action. The Intelligence Reform and Terrorism Prevention Act (IRTPA) of 2004 changed the name of the TTIC to the National Counterterrorism Center (NCTC) and placed it under the direction of the newly created Office of the Director of National Intelligence (ODNI).

A major premise of this thesis is not to deal directly with the intelligence implications collateral to HS duties due to the topic's enormity, however, as previously dictated and in keeping with the thesis argument overlap is inevitable. By law the Office of the Director of National Intelligence (ODNI) directs the efforts of the mega-intelligence fusion center NCTC with a Presidential edict to lead U.S. counter-terrorism efforts, intelligence sharing and integration of national power elements to support CT duties.

Office of the Director of National Intelligence

National Counterterrorism Center (NCTC) a 24-hour, multi-agency staffed, fusion center created by Executive Order 13354 and statutorily authorized functions under the Intelligence Reform and Terrorism Prevention Act (IRTPA) of 2004. The NCTC appears to have lead agency duty for U.S. counter-terrorism efforts, intelligence fusion and sharing, operations coordination and integration of all elements of national power toward those objectives. NCTC is also the repository for the Terrorist Identities Data mart Environment (TIDE), which is the base index storehouse from which the TSC verifies information. The NCTC is statutorily directed to support DHS, DoJ and other law enforcement community of interest stakeholders.

Who Is In Charge?

The problem throughout the paradox of Homeland Security and Homeland Defense is the vastness of not only the problem, but also the diversity of resources and solutions. <u>Organizing all the organizational resources to address HS is crucial to the need for reform elaborated in this thesis.</u> Who does what? DoD, DHS, DoS, DoJ and ODNI as well as other federal agencies all control vast resources, but as demonstrated in this chapter all are charged with similar duties and have overlapping functions. If all the agencies charged with HS/HD are acting independently, then the likelihood that important information or intelligence will be overlooked is almost a certainty. Techniques, processes, and procedures set the structured approach for continual vigilance. Without a common definition, there is no common vision; without clear lines of authority there is no clear delineation of leadership or accountability; and, without a single plan which overarches all the singular efforts of so many in the COI, the enemy has ample opportunity to exploit gaps and seams. The U.S. government must have some indication as to this problem and most assuredly has been provided advice to develop a solution. Chapter 4 will scrutinize research options and recommendations on how to improve comprehensive provision of Homeland Security through National Security reform.

Appendix IV of this thesis is a prima facie, Strength, Weakness, Opportunity and Threat (SWOT) analysis of both the NSC/DoD and the HSC/DHS security/defense organizational models. The fundamental difference between the models appears in two areas; authority and reputation. DoD has the reputation for getting the job done regardless of whether it has the resident core competencies, its strength lies in a history of dependability. DHS is a new agency still establishing itself among federal agencies and must tread carefully and not appear too aggressive, while maintaining assertiveness. DHS must continue to prove itself as an agency capable of leading and protecting. DoD has a cadre of well educated, trained and equipped leaders and employees, bringing a depth of knowledge of how the defense/security process can be adapted to meet difficult objectives. DHS contains an employee base rich in diverse experience and a forward thinking demographic, it is also granted authority to enforce implementation. The DHS methods of implementation are coordination and collaboration. DoD is strong in resource capacity and experience, where DHS lacks the depth of capacity in both areas. DoD lacks the ability or authority to direct or influence domestic implementation of security efforts. DHS has the authority but utilizes a non-directive approach. The models compliment both organizations needs, and a better merging of experience, innovation, authority and competence from both will serve the —whole of government" best.

CHAPTER 4

EVALUATING APPROACHES NATIONAL SECURITY REFORM ARCHETYPES

Goldwater-Nichols Act of 1986

The *Goldwater-Nichols Act of 1986* was a sweeping reform action within DoD that legislatively mandated change to improve the quality of military advice for the President by making the Chairman of the Joint Chiefs (CJCS) the primary military advisor. The Act also placed the Secretary of Defense (SECDEF) in an authoritative position over the Combatant Commanders (COCOMs), to ensure clear authority and responsibility for theatre command was placed squarely with the COCOMs. The Act served to streamline military forces into a collaborative, adaptive, non-politicized organization.

A very important component of the Act was the mandating of joint billets and joint professional education. Joint Professional Military Education (JPME) was a visionary element of the act to enhance officer corps competence, promote synergistic planning, realistic resource acquisition, and practical force management constructs. Lastly, an astute provision of the Act implemented Joint Officer Management to ensure that joint duty career tracts did not affect promotional status of the growing cadre of Joint Staff/Duty Officers (JSO)s.

Following implementation of the Act, military forces were able to recognize the true benefits of economy of effort, and interoperability in mission coordination and equipment acquisition. The successes of joint operations such as Operation Just Cause in Panama, or Operations Desert Shield/Desert Storm in Iraq serve to validate the effectiveness of the joint kinetic operations concept. DoD's paradigm shift was long overdue and the Act resulted in a streamlined military, accountability of theatre commanders, clear and simple chains of command, and a professionalized cadre of military leadership all working within a common framework of thought from which strategic innovation could spring. The Goldwater-Nichols Act of 1986 was the next significant change in the military structure related to NS.

The Goldwater-Nichols Act of 1986 with significant amendments matured the DoD into a joint operational interdependent structure, but the inclusion of the additional elements of national IA power was lacking. Clinton administration SECDEF, William Cohen recognized the deficiencies in IA/DoD integration and sought to improve the NS strategy and processes in order to prepare the nation for the security challenges of the 21st century and beyond. In 1998, he chartered a bi-partisan Commission, which he believed would provide the most comprehensive security analysis since the NSA of 1947."[1]

Hart-Rudman Commission[2]

"And he said, Verily I say unto you, No prophet is accepted in his own country."

Luke 4:24. King James Bible

The *Hart-Rudman Commission*, also known as the *U.S. Commission on National Security/21st Century*, was chartered by the Clinton administration as a bipartisan blue ribbon committee requested to perform a National Security review and assess U.S. needs for the 21st Century. A two and a half year effort by the committee resulted in the issuance of a report in January of 2001 that will go down in history as the most accurate

---

[1] National Security Act of 1947." *National Security Act of 1947* (January 17, 2009): 1. *Academic Search Premier*, EBSCO*host* (accessed March 27, 2010).

[2] United States Commission on National Security/21st Century. *Road Map for National Security : Imperative for Change: the Phase III Report of the U.S. Commission on National Security/21st Century.* The Commission (Washington, D.C.: 2001).

example of ‑*told you so!*"The Commission's report was issued in three parts: Phase I,

entitled: *New World Coming: American Security in the 21st Century,* which examined the

volatile global environment, predicting possible futures and attempting to anticipate

implications to U.S. security posture. Phase II entitled: *Seeking a National Strategy: A*

Concert for Preserving Security and Promoting Freedom, produced a new National

Strategy recommendation to confront the challenges of the predicted future environment.

Lastly, Phase III entitled, *Roadmap for National Security: Imperative for Change,* was a

call for comprehensive National Security reform to implement the objectives of the

proposed strategy. Phase I of the report properly identified the volatility and emergence

of asymmetric warfare and its danger to domestic security. Phase II recognized the

requirement for a strategy which involved unity of effort of the elements of national

power and the community of interest in shielding America against the impending peril.

A quote from *New World Coming: American Security in the 21st Century,* Phase I of the

Hart-Rudman Commission Report is as follows: ‑Americans will likely die on American

soil, possibly in large numbers."[3] Hart-Rudman became more visionary than could be

imagined when eight months prior to 9/11; the report abstractly predicted the critical

attack and the tragic loss of lives on U.S. soil. Phase III of the report included some fifty

recommendations for government reform. Pertinent to the predictive nature of HS are the

recommendations highlighted in this thesis. First and most significant was the

recommendation by the Commission for the President to place Homeland security in

---

[3] United States Commission on National Security/21st Century. *New World Coming American Security in the 21st Century: Major Themes and Implications: the Phase I Report on the Emerging Global Security Environment for the First Quarter of the 21st Century,* The Commission, (Washington, D.C.:1999). 7.

primacy within a new national strategy. The report further called for creation of a

cabinet-level led National Homeland Security Agency (NHSA) with the primary mission

of integrating the planning, prevention, response and recovery efforts of the numerous

entities with Homeland Security responsibilities. Specific recommendations included

restructuring agencies with uniquely HS duties into the NHSA combining agencies like

the Office of National Domestic Preparedness, Federal Emergency Management Agency,

U.S. Customs, U.S. Border Patrol, and the U.S. Coast Guard. Specifically, the report

highlighted the need for integration and coordination of Inter-government organizations

(IGO), Law Enforcement and Non-government organizations (NGO) elements in concert

with business and industry to form a concerted mechanism for provision of security and

adaptive effective response. Within DoD, the recommendations called for creation of a

OSD Assistant Secretary for Homeland Security to oversee DoD activities in homeland

security and for the enhancement of training and equipping the National Guard for duties

and responsibilities as America's primary homeland defense resource. The

recommendations for the NSC included additional members, a return to their essential NS

task rather than foreign policy, and that the NSC coordinate a Presidential directed top-

down strategic planning process and budget to implement the objectives of the developed

strategy. Lastly, the Commission recommended that the President develop an

implementing mechanism to ensure that the reforms contained within the report were

carried out. Purportedly, the report was presented to the Bush administration where it

appears to have been summarily disregarded and the effort of CT analysis and NS review

assigned to Vice President Dick Cheney and national disaster response and coordination

to FEMA.   In fair evaluation of the situation, the NS problems highlighted by Hart-

Rudman existed long before the commission's charter and warnings of domestic peril had gone unheeded before. Enactment of the recommendations in the report would have been subject to the normalcy of Washington bureaucracy and without a precipitating crisis might have continued to remain unaddressed. Many of the recommendations and systemic deficiencies are highlighted in more current reform archetypes such as Beyond Goldwater-Nichols.

Beyond Goldwater- Nichols (BGN)

Beyond Goldwater Nichols (BGN) is a four-year study project completed by the Center for Strategic and International Studies which examined the military, legislative and agency reform requirements to address the systemic problems of national security. This thesis focuses primarily on the recommendations included within phases II and IV as most pertinent to HS. The BGN study teams examined the need for national level security reform based on the change in America's threat environment. BGN's recommendations regarding HS directly reflect the transformation occurring in DoD and IA cultures, which promote a comprehensive approach to NS. The report contains several recommendations beginning with the NSC. The report suggests that the NSC needs to move beyond its traditional and well-accepted role of preparing decisions for the President and take a more active oversight role in National Security policy implementation to guarantee the President's strategic objectives are accomplished at all levels. The report is divided into four phases; a review and synopsis in this chapter will highlight only those most relevant to HS/HD. The Phase I report titled Defense Reform for a New Strategic Era is central to DoD and emphasizes DoD's, Overseas Contingency Operations (OCO) role as war-fighters, ironically as has been pointed out the similarities between OCONUS and domestic problems and solutions are so similar because the problem is a systemic one and the solutions apply to the problem no matter the location or theatre.

Significant, was a recommendation of the report include establishment of a Defense Professional Corps adequately trained and educated through government programs, which allow agencies to mentor and nurture a cadre of professionals. Within the program would be allowance for joint, cross department agency and even non-government assignments endowing the cadre with multi-disciplinary skills. The recommendation also sought the establishment of a 1000 person DoD civilian personnel float in order to ensure the flexibility of DoD to establish the corps of professionals.

The Phase II report titled *U.S. Government and Defense Reform for a New Strategic Era* focused on the IA/DoD interaction or lack of effective interaction. Summarily, the breakdown of the other pertinent recommendations focused on areas such as NS organization's roles and responsibilities, enhancing planning capabilities professional education for military and civilians, and efforts to promote unity of effort. Similar to Hart-Rudman, BGN Phase II also advised of the need for a Quadrennial NS review. The recommendations place onus on the President and the NSC to break down the conventional bureaucracies that have hampered holistic NS solutions by directing roles, responsibilities, and tasks. It further enforces those roles through the direct backing from the White House. As was the case of the National Security Act of 1947 and the Goldwater-Nichols Act of 1986, neither DoD nor the IA will perform this transformation unless directed from the executive level and supported by the legislative.

The Phase III report is entitled *The Future of the National Guard and Reserves*. The gist of the report detailed the need for continued reliance on National Guard and reserve resources as the OPTEMPO of U.S. forces becomes perpetual. The Phase III National Guard Bureau (NGB) recommendations primarily addressed codifying the NGB's role for domestic HD and CS missions .BGN recognized the mission overlap created among IA and DoD and its recommendations will enhance the cooperative relationships already established between NGB assets and the domestic response COI. The study recognizes the need for DoD to embrace the role of the NGB and add primacy to the empowerment and support of NGB efforts through clear delineation of roles and responsibilities. The BGN Phase IV report was constructed in three separate parts*; Invigorating Defense Governance, DoD and the Nuclear Mission of the 21st Century,* and *Managing the Next Domestic Catastrophe*. The majority of recommendations resulting from these portions of the BGN study repeated the suggestions in phases I,II, and III. Emergency response and preparedness were highlighted for reform to ensure inclusion of state and local parties in the COI. Significant, again was a recommendation that echoed those from the Hart-Rudman Commission, calling for the merger of the NSC/HSC, provision of joint planning guidance, building a professional NS education system, and collaborative emergency preparedness and response training. Of note from the study is a primary recommendation to implement a Quadrennial National Security Review (QNSR) to develop interactive national strategic goals to match capabilities with the national strategy. The need for comprehensive NS review has been noted in several recommendations. DoD completed its current QDR for 2010, DHS completed its QHSR for 2010, the Department of State's (DoS) Quadrennial Diplomacy and Development

Review (QDDR), although has not been completed as of this writing. BGN also directed development of a classified national security planning guidance in each administration's 1st year to set NS objectives for the government. At the time of this writing, the current administration has not published a National Security Strategy (NSS) document; it is past due, and sorely needed. Lack of alacrity in releasing this document leaves the NS apparatus to infer Commander-in Chief's intent from White House actions, speeches and other information. The conclusions and recommendations of the BGN study emphasize that the executive branch must direct comprehensive National Security reform and it must be supported by the legislative branch and were based on the study of Goldwater-Nichols effectiveness, the current volatility and non-predictive threat environment and the efficacy of the current systems that accomplish NS.

Project for National Security Reform (PNSR)

Based on a congressional mandate and with the support of the Center for the Study of the Presidency, the Project for National Security Reform (PNSR) completed one of the most extensive reviews of National Security in history. The PNSR 800 page report *Forging A New Shield* was released in December 2008. It reviewed the history of NS, the previous attempts at review and reform, the threat environment and the forces that act to disrupt a comprehensive NS effort. Although the major premise of the study as well as many of the participants were the same as those from the BGN study, PNSR reaches further into the NS problem, properly placing the context into a construct of complex and interdependent systems dependent upon internal manageable and external unmanageable forces. Furthermore, the follow-up PNSR study entitled, *Turning Ideas Into Action,* released in September 2009 is the PNSR's amended recommendations of the initial study and guidance to the administration and Congress based on current circumstances to initiate change in the NS structure. As with many of the recommendations of the Hart-Rudman Commission, ad-hoc implementation of several recommendations from the PNSR studies has already occurred within the NS COI. This section will provide an overall view of the recommendations as delineated in Appendix 5 of *Turning Ideas Into Action*[4]. The study grouped the initial and current recommendations into eight categories and definitive objectives to accomplish the overall strategy.

> NEW APPROACHES BASED ON NATIONAL MISSIONS AND OUTCOMES: Reform the national security system to establish strategic end-to-end management processes and achieve overall integrated effort, collaboration, and agility.
>
> STRATEGY DEVELOPMENT AND PLANNING GUIDANCE: Develop a national security strategy and accompanying planning and resource guidance for the interagency system.
>
> ALIGNMENT OF STRATEGY AND RESOURCES: Link resources to goals through national security mission-based analysis and budgeting.
>
> INTERAGENCY TEAMS AND TASK FORCES: Delegate and unify management of national security issues and missions through empowered interagency and intergovernmental teams and crisis task forces.
>
> INTERAGENCY AND INTERGOVERNMENTAL TEAMS FOR HOMELAND SECURITY: Create an integrated federal, state, local, territorial, and tribal homeland security and emergency management system
>
> HUMAN CAPITAL: Align personnel incentives, leader development, personnel preparation, and organizational culture with strategic objectives.
>
> KNOWLEDGE AND INTELLECTUAL CAPITAL: Greatly improve the flow of knowledge and information.
>
> CONGRESSIONAL RESPONSIBILITIES: Create mechanisms for the oversight and resourcing of integrated national missions.

---

[4] James R. Locher III , et al., *Project on National Security Reform: Turning Ideas Into Action* Center for the Study of the Presidency, Appendix 5, (Arlington, VA: September 2009) 205-236.

The PNSR is farsighted in that its systematic approach begins with placing emphasis for transformation squarely where it belongs, with the President and supported by Congress. The defining of the NS mission as inclusive of Homeland Security, Homeland Defense, Emergency Preparedness and Response and Civil Support will provide an all hazards solution with clearly defined missions, goals and objectives aligned with the National Security Strategy. Defining agency roles and responsibilities will set the stage for an adaptive, responsive, multi-disciplined agency, which cross functionally incorporates collaborative efforts across the NS spectrum, including stakeholder input at all levels of the COI. Provision for expansion of the professional NS personnel cadre, knowledge base, training, and competency will allow for the best and the brightest to be the watch standers in an ever-evolving fight. Integration has been the intent since the NSA of 1947 and the call for a new NS Act will provide for the creation of agency, mission strategic planning, and resourcing of the international and domestic aspects of NS security. The reforms contained within the PNSR recommendations address the seams and gaps symbolic of the unorganized chaos of current efforts and self-imposed boundaries.

CHAPTER 5

RECOMMENDATIONS

The nature of this thesis has evolved from concentration on Homeland Security and Homeland Defense to National Security, simply because they are all the same and the actions and statements of the present administration validate that evolution. In Presidential Security Directive-1 (PSD-1), President Obama stated:

> I believe that Homeland Security is indistinguishable from National Security – conceptionally and functionally, they should be thought of together rather than separately. Instead of separating these issues we must create an integrated effective and efficient approach to enhance the National Security of the United States."[5]

Based on the Obama administration's actions, it appears that a fundamental change of thought regarding NS/HS and HD is occurring, which implies that division is not effective, and collaboration is. Recognizing that separation of the NS/HD/HS duties was part of the problem is vital in implementing reform. There is an old idiom that says the more *cooks, the worse potage* roughly paraphrased is best expressed in another idiom-*too many cooks spoil the soup.* This administration gets the message, the threat is not the prevalent problem, it is the largess and disorganization of the myriad concurrent solutions that is the problem. Systemic failure in connecting the dots of NS is the result of too many seams and gaps left uncovered as was expressed by the White House following the December 25, 2009 underwear bomber attempt in Detroit.

---

[5] Barack H. Obama. *Organizing for Homeland Security and Terrorism.* Presidential Study Directive-1(PSD-1), (Washington D.C.: 2009). 1 and 2. (accessed at http://www.fas.org/irp/offdocs/psd/psd-1.pdf on January 15, 2010).

From Many, One

The first positive step toward NS reform was taken by the Obama administration in May of 2009; it has brought the advisory function of HS under the umbrella of NS and is attempting to remove the barriers that have long existed between the two functions. The restructuring of the Homeland Security Council and the National Security Council into the National Security Staff (NSS) is a foundational step in National Security reform. The NSA of 1947 planted the seeds for integration of the IA and the military machine, but the concept never matured. NS reform will nurture that interaction and allow the growth and innovation that will produce a viable comprehensive solution, which includes the efforts, plans, and capabilities of the COI. NS reform has the potential to transform the disjunctive HS/HD into a shield of integrated processes, systems, plans and coordinated responses to defend America in depth and it begins with a common definition leading to a common goal. What is needed is a new National Security Act to define the problem, identify the objective, assign responsibility, develop the plan, resources and mechanisms to accomplish National Security.

One Definition

As noted industrialist and philanthropist Andrew Carnegie,[6] who knew a thing or two about success once said, "Teamwork is the ability to work together toward a common vision." The variety of definitions illustrated in Chapter One are by no means inclusive of the myriad interpretations that exist across the spectrum of Homeland Security/Defense. A common definition of HS/HD is non-existent, yet the singular

---

[6] Biography.com, Andrew Carnegie (accessed February 27, 2010, from Biography.com at http://www.biography.com/articles/Andrew-Carnegie-9238756).

definitions each have collateral equity. These collateral equities grant commonality of purpose to HD and HS as functions of National Security. How apparent is, it to even a layman that the commonalities of threat, response and jurisdictions dictate that Homeland Security and Homeland Defense functions of National Security be directly managed as parts of the same mission. Having thus conceded the enormity and complexity of comprehensive NS, the first task is to begin scoping it into manageable portions and functions. The National Security problem is an elephant eaten one bite at a time by many mouths. National Security reform should therefore begin with one definition, leading to one solution, provided by many. From many definitions, one common vision for success.

One Plan

The National Security Strategy (NSS), the National Defense Strategy (NDS), the FBI National Strategic Plan, and the National Strategy for Homeland Security (NSHS) all strategically direct HS/HD/CT efforts through policy guidance. There is no single enveloping plan that effectively incorporates all NS efforts for the prevention and disruption of terrorist attacks. Each agency works independently; numerous task forces work without knowledge of operational overlap, often performing redundant tasks and providing similar products. As demonstrated in Chapter Four, there are numerous Operation Centers (OC) charged with integrating intelligence and operations across the community of interest. OCs have evolved into situational awareness, and reporting mechanisms bereft of operational influence. The NCTC which was created from the recommendations of the 9/11 Commission, collaboratively developed the *National Implementation Plan for the War on Terror* which encompasses strategic planning among the elements of power, but it does not coordinate the day-to-day operational efforts of the

NS apparatus. Without constant monitoring and adjustment, the interdependent NS structure falters and fails to grow.

However, not all is lost, as vast progress in providing comprehensive emergency preparedness and responses have occurred. Emergency preparedness and response are certainly key elements in providing comprehensive protection of domestic U.S. interest. Statutorily, DHS is charged with the development of the mechanism to provide integrated Emergency Preparedness (EP) and Emergency Response (ER). The singular document that facilitates combined response at all levels of the elements of national power and combined with state, local, and non-governmental organizations is the National Response Framework (NRF). Astoundingly this document provides doctrine, structure, roles and responsibilities, and provides for the planning and exercise and evaluation requirements of the contingency and crisis action plans associated with catastrophic domestic incidents. The NRF coordinates efforts from the initial first responder through the full federal response from the community of interest.

If the construct of the NRF facilitates national response across functions, preserves equities and incorporates state, local and non-governmental organizations, it should be adopted on a grander scale to manage the National Security Framework. Group the task of NS into Military Missions, Intelligence, Law Enforcement, and Diplomatic Missions, all of which interactively provide comprehensive national security. The Multi-Agency Coordination Systems (MACS) within NIMS are viable as National Security Management constructs for functions of HD/HS due to their widespread familiarity and proven functionality. Each of those functions can be overseen by the appropriate lead agency and coordinated locally via the same channels used during emergency response, with tasking among Operation Centers coordinated and leveraged for maximum fusion and efficacy. Contingency Plans and crisis action plans can be shared to the degree applicable and best use of available resources applied in the day-to-day management of national security. Cross functionality breeds diverse competence and effectiveness and from many plans, there can emerge one coordinated response.

One Agency

The NSC was created from the NSA of 1947 to integrate and focus the efforts of the DoD and the IA. The problem in that construct was the boundary it created rather than removed. The U.S. Government is the IA! The NSA, while successful in initializing change in DoD structure and encouraging interaction of non-DoD organizations like the CIA, never really included the rest of the U.S. government. What might have been accomplished if DoS had been resourced to the same extent as DoD in its National Security roles since WWII, what of USAID and its constant under-funding? The lack of unity and inter-agency inclusion in the planning process led to the current situation. Certainly, the case is made for viability of agencies like USAID that can provide needed reconstruction and stability missions, relieving DoD of shouldering the complete post hostilities burden.

U.S. war-fighters fight wars and prepare for transition to those organizations (DoD, DHS, UN…) with the assumed capability to enable conditions for resumption of stable civil authority and facilitating the desired strategic end states. Why then do we not provide that competent relief of function to DoD by the IA? The NRF and ICS systems provide for competencies and capacity to fill the needs for reconstruction, stabilization, and support of civil authorities following catastrophic events. Many of those competencies are useful following post-hostility kinetic actions; making the NRF a possible resource for identifying Civilian Response Corps resources. Because we also provide "clean-up on aisle four" after the war is done, U.S. forces now operate with restraints that dictate that they annihilate enemies, while being careful not to destroy anything significant along the way. U.S. forces are also guaranteed prolonged missions due to lack of planning for phase IV and V, termination or transition actions. This set of circumstances influences HS in that it ties up U.S. forces in perpetual conflict, leaving minimal emphasis on protecting the homeland. The fight may begin OCONUS but the most experienced strategist knows you do not leave your flanks exposed.

One agency (DoD) with multiple integrated components was the result of reorganization begun in 1947 and further fostered in 1986. Integrated organizational maturation must continue toward completion. The NCTC is charged by law to integrate the CT effort but its discipline remains heavily weighted in intelligence vice operations. Joint planning constructs and multi-agency constructs from DoD and DHS respectively afford us the ability to fuse cultures, planning and ideas. The Joint Inter-Agency Coordination Group is quite similar to the Unified Coordination Group under the NIMS construct. HD/Defense Coordination Officers (DCO)s and HS/Federal Coordination Officers (FCO)s perform similar duties. Dysfunctional and redundant organizational functions within the current NS/HS/HD model must be managed and integrated. What is needed is a system, which removes the "us versus them" type of labeling between the IA and DoD, after all, the players in that pool are paid by the same government. Joint duty assignments and fellowships should be encouraged throughout the NS COI. Joint duties in the NS realm should include non-deprecating, cross-functional assignment between IA and DoD structures. Joint duty should reflect assignments other than duty at OSD, the

Pentagon or deployed with another military service. Joint duty assignments may reveal similarities and equities not readily apparent and could possibly lead to a cadre of pre-trained IA personnel with CSRS capabilities.

A Unified Command or Multi-Agency Command does not detract from any authority of the organizations, which work within it. Unity of effort is nationally and to a lesser extent internationally effective in prosecuting wars, managing catastrophic incident response and in crisis action planning and operations, but is not used for the day-to-day integration of National Security processes. Perhaps we should step out of the forest and view the trees. From many entities, the NS community of interest must transform into one community of action.

One Leader

Chapter Five confirmed the number of legislative, academic, and historic solutions that have attempted to address the problem of comprehensive NS. Even with legislation, doctrine and the blood of innocents killed by terrorists on 9/11, no significant change has occurred until recently. Noted British conservative statesman, Sir Edmund Burke is attributed to have stated: ―All that is necessary for the triumph of evil is for good men to do nothing."[7] America sits content after each foiled attempt, misled that we are doing all that we can in the war on terrorism until the next successful attack. The December 2009 underwear bomber exposed the gaps and seams that exist not only in physical security but also in screening procedures and processes and in our lack of

---

[7] Encyclopedia Britannica Online, Edmund Burke in *Encyclopedia Britannica*. (accessed February 27, 2010 from: http://www.britannica.com/EBchecked/topic/85362/Edmund-Burke).

emphasis on identifying possible terrorist actors. President Obama stated in his response to the American people following the incident that:

> In short, we need our intelligence, homeland security and law enforcement systems -- and the people in them -- to be accountable and to work as intended: collecting, sharing, integrating, analyzing, and acting on intelligence as quickly and effectively as possible to save innocent lives -- not just most of the time, but all the time. That's what the American people deserve.[8]

The president's statement was strong and might well inspire a sense of well-being that the systems will work together in the future. What is needed is more than a statement, what is needed is National Security reform that cuts through bureaucracies, empowers change, encourages fusion and allows us to cover the gaps and seal the seams in such a way that incidents like the 25 December 2009 attempt will become an anomaly.

NS reform also implies providing mechanisms, which prepare the NS COI to better interact and perform. One such mechanism is joint education, a system of National Security education for NS professionals similar to the Professional Military Education system is a prerequisite to developing an informed COI. If the interdependent functions of the NS system are to act in concert, then it must be educated in concert. Both the Beyond Goldwater-Nichols study and the Project for National Security Reform study advocate a system of education and assignments to produce a cadre of educated, informed, and highly competent National Security professionals. The suggestion recommending that current systems such as the National Defense University System could be transformed into a National Security University and include curricula that

---

[8] The White House, Office of the Press Secretary, For Immediate Release: Release *Remarks by the President on Security Reviews*, January 05, 2010. (Washington D.C.2010) (accessed at http://www.whitehouse.gov/the_press_office/remarks-by-the-president-on-a-new-strategy-for-afghanistan-and-pakistan/ on January 12, 2010).

provide education regarding IA processes relating to NS is a perfect example of visionary solutions for today's problems. When NS education is the norm throughout the COI, then "All Will Learn as One" will truly make it possible that "All May Labor as One."[9] The diverse interactions of NS students will profit the community of interest with the innovation and ingenuity which miscellany allows. President Obama must lead, push, and promote reform that encompasses integration of form, fit and function into one totality of effort.

One Answer

The Obama administration has recognized the lack of unity of purpose and has begun directing a more cohesive NS effort; Appendix V is an example of the merger of the NSC and HSC into the National Security Staff to address the problem geographically, functionally and with diverse input from the COI stakeholders. The answer to the question posed at the beginning of this thesis was, "Who does what and to whom?" The answer to that question appears to be that everyone is attempting to do everything, all at the same time. All those entities working in unorganized chaos, is the singular problem. Comprehensive National Security reform is the single answer.

---

[9] Motto of the NDU, Joint Forces Staff College

CHAPTER 6

CONCLUSION

This thesis has exposed the lack of commonality in defining Homeland Security and Homeland Defense while highlighting the commonalities of the two missions. Previous chapters uncovered the diversity of the threat and the magnitude of managing a comprehensive solution to the problem of HS/HD. The contents of this document led to the identification of the numerous entities with mission overlap and varied capabilities all working independently and in some cases redundantly. The continued exploitation of the seam of uncertainty, diverse efforts, and lack of commonality is evidenced in daily incidents that highlight an inability to present a secure domestic posture. Lastly, study was conducted of the pre-eminent suggestions regarding reform of the ―system" of administrative and operational endeavors responsible for providing not Homeland, but National Security.

The title of this thesis, *E Pluribus Unum* did not become apparent until the end of the research. The problem clearly stated is this: the global threat of extremist violence is a common problem that has a deadly price if improperly addressed. The use of terrorism as an element of war by non-state actors who have the ability, network, resources, and the will to wreak unimaginable havoc is a problem that no single nation or agency can address alone. DoD resources are stretched to the limit in perpetual kinetic actions abroad. DoS faces increasing numbers of regions in imminent conflict. DHS, still in its infancy as an agency, battles dwindling funding, multifarious threats, and multifaceted coordination issues. The current administration has committed to a strategy, which sustains efforts to build in our partner countries the ability to protect themselves, advance democracy, and rid themselves of violent extremists and in doing so provide the U.S. and the world a measure of comfort from illicit attacks. As in any war, however, the enemy has a vote and in this instance that vote will be to strike at America in ways we have yet to imagine. *The question remains not if the next attack will occur but when....truly when?*

The nature of war has never changed; it remains the imposition of one's will upon another through the use of force. The basis of the imposed will may be political, economic, ideological, or simply psychotic tyranny. The violent imposition of will is now so widely diverse and changing in character and direction that it is impossible to guard against completely. The solution advocated in this thesis involves reform, which accentuates collaboration not command and adaptation of concepts already in existence. As was expressed by President Obama, HS is NS, and the two are a singular mission. The disconnect resulting from over-eager operational response to provide NS is the cause of the vulnerability to the National Security System. Past legislation has sought to address the lack of collaborative efforts in the NS community and has failed. Without a common foundation, the efforts of the many NS/HS and HS agencies are useless. The variety of jurisdictions and ―Operations Centers" demonstrate the lack of mutual effort and leads to inefficiency within NS. The lack of common terminology, minimal unity of effort and absence of a comprehensive vision are symptomatic of an interdependent although dysfunctional system. The current administration has begun the process of studying the NS system and implementing corrections. The success of those efforts will be proven in the future. What is most important is that the impetus was needed and it had to be driven from the executive level. The cultural change in IA collaborative processes

97

emphasizes pursuance of cooperative national security that encompasses the critical competencies and capabilities of military, civilian, coalition and non-government partners.

The enterprise concept elaborated in the 2010 QHSR is indicative of a change in perspective and methodology; diverse stakeholders participate based on common goals, which contribute to the overall success. Successful protection of America can only be obtained through the commitment and sustained cooperation of the community of interest over the full range of national security initiatives. The NS COI must present a single shield of protection so dense as to provide defense-in-depth which discourages all who would seek to do us harm. With National Security reform: out of many different nations, agencies, organizations, jurisdictions, plans and responses, will emerge one structure, one plan, one team effort and America will be safe again! If we do not act on National Security reform, what happens the next time we hear? *—We have some planes.....*[1]"

---

[1] *FAA audio file, Boston Center, position 46R, 8:24:38 and 8:24:56;Peter Zalewski interview (Sept. 23, 2003) in the The 9/11 Commission Report: Final Report of the National Commission on Terrorist Attacks Upon the United States.(New York: Norton, 2004). As cited on pages 10 and 455.*

BIBLIOGRAPHY

National Security Reform Recommendations

Center for Strategic and International Studies. *Beyond Goldwater-Nichols: Defense Reform for a New Strategic Era, Phase 1 Report*. Arlington, VA.: March, 2004.

Center for Strategic and International Studies. *Beyond Goldwater-Nichols: U.S. Government and Defense Reform for a New Strategic Era, Phase 2 Report*. Arlington, VA.: July 2005.

Center for Strategic and International Studies. *Beyond Goldwater-Nichols:* The Future of the National Guard and Reserves, *Phase 3 Report*. Arlington, VA.: July 2006.

Center for Strategic and International Studies. *Commission on Smart Power: A Smarter, More Secure America*. Arlington, VA.: 2007.

Center for Strategic and International Studies. *Invigorating Defense Governance: A Beyond Goldwater-Nichols Phase 4 Report*. Arlington, VA.: March 2008.

Center for the Study of the Presidency. *Project on National Security Reform: Preliminary Findings*. Arlington, VA: July 2008.

Center for the Study of the Presidency. *Project on National Security Reform: Forging a New Shield*. Arlington, VA: November 2008.

Center for the Study of the Presidency. *Project on National Security Reform: Case Studies Volume I*. Arlington, VA.: 2008.

Locher, James, R. III, et al., *Project on National Security Reform: Turning Ideas Into Action*. Center for the Study of the Presidency. Arlington, VA: 2009.

Murdock, Clark and David R. Scruggs, —*Beyond Goldwater-Nichols: An Annotated Brief* Center for Strategic and International Studies." Arlington, VA: August 1, 2004. http://csis.org/publication/beyond-goldwater-nichols-annotaed-brief (accessed September 13, 2009).

Murdock, Clark et al. *Beyond Goldwater-Nichols Phase I Report: Defense Reform for a New Strategic Era* Center for Strategic and International Studies. March, 2004. http://csis.org/publication/beyond-goldwater-nichols-phase-i-report (accessed September 13, 2009).

Murdock, Clark et al. *Invigorating Defense Governance: A Beyond Goldwater-Nichols Phase 4 Report* | Center for Strategic and International Studies. March 2008. http://csis.org/publication/invigorating-defense-governance (accessed September 13, 2009).

National Commission on Terrorist Attacks upon the United States. *Final Report of the National Commission on Terrorist Attacks Upon the United States, The 9-11 Commission Report*. U.S. G.P.O. Washington D.C.:2004.

United States Commission on National Security/21st Century. *New World Coming American Security in the 21st Century: Major Themes and Implications: the Phase I Report on the Emerging Global Security Environment for the First Quarter of the 21st Century*. The Commission, Washington, D.C.: 1999.

United States Commission on National Security/21st Century. *Road Map for National Security Imperative for Change: the Phase III Report of the U.S. Commission on National Security/21st Century*. The Commission, Washington, D.C.: 2001.

United States Commission on National Security/21st Century. *Seeking a National Strategy A Concert for Preserving Security and Promoting Freedom: the Phase II Report on U.S. National Security Strategy for the 21st Century*. The Commission, Washington, D.C.: 2000.

Presidential Directives and Publications

Bush, George W. ─Homeland Security Presidential Directive-1 (HSPD-1). *"Organization and Operation of the Homeland Security Council."* Washington, D.C.: October 29, 2001. Federation of American Scientists. http://www.fas.org/ irp/offdocs/nspd/hspd-1.htm (accessed September 13, 2009).

Bush, George W. "Executive Order 13440--Interpretation of the Geneva Conventions Common Article 3 as Applied to a Program of Detention and Interrogation Operated by the Central Intelligence Agency." *Weekly Compilation of Presidential Documents"* 43, no. 30 (July 30, 2007): 1000-1002. *Academic Search Elite*, EBSCO*host* (accessed March 27, 2010).

Bush, George W. Homeland Security Presidential Directive-1(HSPD-1). ─*Organization and Operation of the Homeland Security Council*." White House, Washington, D.C.: October 29, 2001.

Bush, George W. Homeland Security Presidential Directive-5(HSPD-5). "*Directive on Management of Domestic Incidents*." February 28, 2003. *Weekly Compilation of Presidential Documents* 39, no. 10 (March 10, 2003): 280. *Academic Search Premier*, EBSCO*host* (accessed March 27, 2010)..

Bush, George W. Homeland Security Presidential Directive-8 (HSPD-8). *"National Preparedness*." White House Office of the Press Secretary, Washington, D.C.: December 17, 2003.

Bush, George W. National Security Presidential Directive No. 51 (NSPD-51). *"National Continuity Policy.* and Homeland Security Presidential Directive-20. White House, Washington, D.C.: April 4, 2007.

Bush, George W. National Security Presidential Directive-1(NSPD-1). *"Organization of the National Security Council System."* Washington, D.C.: February 13, 2001. http://www.fas.org/irp/offdocs/nspd/nspd-1.htm (accessed September 13, 2009).

Obama, Barack H. Presidential Memorandum. "Memorandum on the Attempted Terrorist Attack on December 25, 2009: *Intelligence, Screening, and Watch listing System Corrective Actions." Daily Compilation of Presidential Documents* (January 7, 2010): 1-3. *Academic Search Premier*, EBSCO*host* (accessed March 27, 2010).

Obama, Barack H. Presidential Policy Directive-1 (PPD-1) *Organization of the National Security Council System."* Washington, D.C.: February 13, 2009.

Obama, Barack H. Presidential Study Directive-1(PSD-1), *Organizing for Homeland Security and Terrorism."* Washington D.C.: February 23, 2009.

U.S. President. Executive Order. *National Security Professional Development, Executive Order 13434 of May 17, 2007."* Federal Register 72, no. 98. Washington D.C.: May 22, 2007.

U.S. President. National Security Presidential Directive-1 (NSPD-1). *Organization of the National Security Council System."* The White House, Washington, D.C.: February, 13 2001.

U.S. President. National Security Presidential Directive-44 (NSPD-44). *Management of Interagency Efforts Concerning Reconstruction and Stabilization."* The White House, Washington D.C: December 7, 2005.

National Security Strategies, Reviews and Joint Publications

Department of Defense. *Joint Publication 1: Doctrine for the Armed Forces of the United States."* Washington, D.C.: May 14, 2007. http://www.dtic.mil/ doctrine/jel/new_pubs/jp1.pdf (accessed September 13, 2009).

Department of Defense. *Joint Publication 3: Joint Operations."* Washington, D.C.: 2006, September with change 1, 2008, February. http://www.dtic.mil/ doctrine/jel/new_pubs/jp3_0.pdf (accessed September 13, 2009).

Gates, Robert Michael. *Quadrennial Defense Review Report."* Dept. of Defense, Washington, D.C.: 2010.

Homeland Security Council (U.S.), and United States. *National Strategy for Homeland Security."* The White House, Washington, D.C.: 2002.

Interagency Counterinsurgency Initiative (U.S.). *—U.S. Government Counterinsurgency Guide.*" United States Government Interagency Counterinsurgency Initiative, Washington, D.C.: 2009.

Napolitano, Janet. *"Quadrennial Homeland Security Review Report."* Department of Homeland Security, Washington D.C.: 2010.

Rumsfeld, Donald. *_Quadrennial Defense Review Report.*' Washington, D.C.: Dept. of Defense, 2006.

The White House. *—National Security Strategy of the United States of America.*" White House, Washington, D.C.: March 2006.

United States. *—Department of Defense Homeland Security Joint Operating Concept Version 2.0.*" Strategy Division (J5S), USNORTHCOM: Peterson AFB, Colo: 2007.

United States. *—Interagency, Intergovernmental Organization, and Nongovernmental Organization Coordination During Joint Operations, Vol. I.*" Joint Chiefs of Staff, Washington, D.C.: 2006.

United States. *—Interagency, Intergovernmental Organization, and Nongovernmental Organization Coordination During Joint Operations Vol II.*" Joint Chiefs of Staff, Washington, D.C.: 2006.

United States. *—National Defense Strategy.*" Department of Defense, Washington D.C.: 2008.

United States. *—National Defense Strategy.*" Dept. of Defense Washington, D.C.: 2008.

United States. *—National Military Strategy of the United States of America 2004, a Strategy for Today; a Vision for Tomorrow.*" Joint Chiefs of Staff, Washington, DC: 2004.

United States. *—National Response Plan.*" Dept. of Homeland Security, Washington DC: 2004.

United States. *—One Team, One Mission, Securing Our Homeland U.S. Department of Homeland Security Strategic Plan, Fiscal Years 2008-2013.*" The Department, Washington, D.C.: 2008.

United States. *—The National Military Strategy of the United States of America A Strategy for Today, a Vision for Tomorrow.*" Joint Chiefs of Staff, Washington, D.C.: 2004.

United States. *—The National Security Strategy of the United States of America.*" Executive Office of the President, Washington, D.C.: 2002.

United States. Joint Publication, 3-27. "Homeland Defense." Joint Chiefs of Staff, Washington, DC: 2007.

Books

Bensahel, Nora and Anne M. Moisan. "Repairing the Interagency Process." *Joint Force Quarterly*, no. 44 (1st Quarter 2007): 106.

Binnendijk, Hans and Stuart E. Johnson, eds. *Transforming for Stabilization and Reconstruction Operations*. Washington, D.C.: National Defense University Press, 2004.

Binnendijk, Hans, ed. *Transforming America's Military*. Washington, DC: National Defense University Press, 2002.

Buchanan, Jeffrey, Maxie Davis, and Lee Wight. "Death of the Combatant Command? Toward a Joint Interagency Approach." *Joint Force Quarterly*, no. 52 (1st Quarter 2009): 92-96.

Buck, Peter D. *The Iranian Hostage Rescue Attempt: A Case Study*. Masters Thesis, Quantico, VA: U.S. Marine Corps Command and Staff College, December 4, 2002.

Carafano, James. "Missions, Responsibilities, and Geography: Rethinking How the Pentagon Commands the World." *Backgrounder*, no. 1792 (August 2004): 1-5. 113.

Cronin, Patrick M. *Global Strategic Assessment 2009: America's Security Role in a Changing World*. Washington, D.C.: Published for the Institute for National Strategic Studies by the National Defense University Press, 2009.

Desai, Sunil B. "Solving the Interagency Puzzle: The Lessons of Jointness." *Policy Review*, no. 129 (February & March 2005): 57-72.

Friedberg, Aaron L. "Strengthening U.S. Strategic Planning." *The Washington Quarterly* (Winter 2007-2008): 47-60.

Gardner, Jeffrey V. "Fight the _Away Game' as a Team: Organizing for Regional Interagency Policy Implementation." *American Intelligence Journal* (Autumn/Winter 2005): 51-60.

Gates, Robert M. "The National Defense Strategy: Striking the Right Balance." *Joint Force Quarterly*, no. 52 (1st Quarter 2009).

Locher, James R. *Victory on the Potomac: The Goldwater-Nichols Act Unifies the Pentagon*. College Station: Texas A&M University Press, 2002.

Magnus, Ralph H., and Eden Naby. *Afghanistan: Mullah, Marx, and Mujahid*. Boulder, Colo: Westview Press, 1998.

Mansfield, Laura. *His Own Words: Translation and Analysis of the Writings of Dr. Ayman Al Zawahiri*. Old Tappan, NJ: TLG Publications, 2006.

Murdock, Clark A., and Richard W. Weitz. "Beyond Goldwater--Nichols." *JFQ: Joint Force Quarterly* no. 38 (Summer2005 2005): 34-41. *Academic Search Premier*, EBSCO*host* (accessed March 27, 2010).

Nye, Joseph S. Jr. *Soft Power: The Means to Success in World Politics*. New York: Public Affairs, 2004.

Professional Journals, Reports, Magazines and Articles

RAND Corporation. Hunter, Robert Edwards, *Integrating Instruments of Power and Influence: Lessons Learned and Best Practices.* http://www.rand.org, 2008. (accessed December 12, 2009)

Ricks, Thomas E. *Fiasco: The American Military Adventure in Iraq.* New York: The Penguin Press, 2006.

Rife, Rickey L. ―Defense is From Mars State is From Venus.: Improving Communications and Promoting National Security." College Fellow Research monograph, United States Army War College, Carlisle, PA. May, 1998.

Said, Sami and Cameron G. Holt. ―A Time for Action: The Case for Interagency Deliberate Planning." *Strategic Studies Quarterly* (Fall 2008): 30-71.

United States Institute of Peace. *The Iraq Study Group Report* (2006).

Van Opdorp, Harold. ―The Joint Interagency Coordination Group: The Operationalization of DIME." *Small Wars Journal* Volume 2 (July 2005): 1-12.

White Paper on PDD/NSC 56 Managing Complex Contingency Operations. Washington, DC: Federation of American Scientists, (May,1997).

Woodward, Bob. *State of Denial.* New York: Simon and Schuster, 2006.

Zinni, Anthony and Tony Koltz. *The Battle for Peace: A Frontline Vision of America's Power and Purpose.* New York: Palgrave Macmillan, 2006.

Government Publications

Congressional Research Service Report for Congress RL34253. *Weak and Failing States: Evolving Security Threats and U.S.Policy*, by Liana Sun Wyler. Congressional Research Service. Washington, DC, updated April 2008.

Congressional Research Service Report for Congress RL34455, *Organizing the U.S. Government for National Security: Overview of the Interagency Reform Debates*, by Catherine Dale, Nina Serafino and Pat Towell. Congressional Research Service. Washington, DC, April, 2008.

Congressional Research Service Report for Congress RL34505. *National Security Strategy: Legislative Mandates, Execution to Date, and Considerations for Congress*, by Catherine Dale. Congressional Research Service. Washington, DC, July 2008.

Congressional Research Service Report for Congress RL34565. *Building an Interagency Cadre of National Security Professionals: Proposals, Recent Experience, and Issues for Congress*, by Catherine Dale. Congressional Research Service. Washington, DC, July 2008.

Congressional Research Service Report for Congress, *Peacekeeping/Stabilization and Conflict Transitions: Background and Congressional Action on the Civilian Response/Reserve Corps and other Civilian Stabilization and Reconstruction Capabilities*, by Nina Serafino and Martin Weiss. Congressional Research Service. Washington, DC, September, 2008.

Homeland Security Act of 2002. U.S. Government Printing Office, Washington, D.C.:2002.

International Narcotics Control Board. *Report of the International Narcotics Control Board for 2008*. United Nations,New York: 2009.

National Security Act of 1947. *National Security Act of 1947* (January 17, 2009): *Academic Search Premier*, EBSCO*host* (accessed March 27, 2010).

United States. *Joint Resolution to Authorize the Use of United States Armed Forces against Those Responsible for the Recent Attacks Launched against the United States*. U.S. G.P.O., Washington, D.C.: 2001.

United States. *Narco-Terrorism: International Drug Trafficking and Terrorism, a Dangerous Mix : Hearing Before the Committee on the Judiciary, United States Senate, One Hundred Eighth Congress, First Session, May 20, 2003*. U.S. G.P.O., Washington D.C.: 2003.

United States. *National Security Act of 1947*. Washington, D.C.: U.S. GPO, 1957.

United States. *White Paper of the Interagency Policy Group's Report on U.S. Policy Toward Afghanistan and Pakistan*. Washington, D.C.: March, 2009.

Websites

ABC news.com, Richard Esposito and Brian Ross. *Investigators: Northwest Bomb Plot Planned by al Qaeda in Yemen*, 2009 at /The blotter from Brian Ross website article. (accessed at http://abcnews.go.com/Blotter/al-qaeda-yemen-planned-northwest-flight-253-bomb-plot/story?id=9426085 on December 26, 2009).

Associated Press News and Information Research Center, "*List of Foiled Terror Plots,*" *Newsday,* June 2, 2007, at *www.newsday.com/news/local/newyork/am-foiledplots0603,0,7211531.story?coll=ny-main-breakingnewslinks,*October 19, 2007. Accessed through The Heritage Foundation website , article by James Jay Carafano, Ph.D. *U.S. Thwarts 19 Terrorist Attacks Against America Since 9/11,* November 13 2007. http://www.heritage.org/Research/HomelandDefense/bg2085.cfm (accessed December 5, 2009).

Boston.com, Pamela Constable. Washington Post accessed from internet Boston Globe website, Boston.com/ *5 US ,jihadists" saythey weren't planning attacks.* Http://www.boston.com/news/world/asia/articles/2010/01/05/5_us_jihadists_say_they_werent_planning_attacks/ (accessed January 5, 2010).

CNN.com/US website article, Andy Brooks and Catherine Quayle, *Terror on Trial: Timothy McVeigh executed,* December 31, 2007. http://www.cnn.com/2007/US/law/12/17/court.archive.mcveigh/index.html#cnnSTCText. (accessed February 10,2010).

Federal Bureau of Investigation website, Headline Archives, The Year In Review- *A Look at FBI Cases, Part 1*, http://www.fbi.gov/page2/dec09/review_122809.html, (accessed March 02, 2009).

U.S. Government. —National Security Professional Development." National Security Professional Development Program. http://www.nspd.gov. (accessed September 7, 2005).

Statements

107TH Congress, 2D Sessions, S. Rept. NO. 107- 351 H. Rept. NO. 107-792, page 6, *Report of The Joint Inquiry Into The Terrorist Attacks Of September 11, 2001 – By The House Permanent Select Committee On Intelligence And The Senate Select Committee On Intelligence. Washington D.C.:* December 2002. (accessed at http://www.gpoaccess.gov/serialset/creports/pdf/fullreport_errata.pdf on January 6, 2010.

Department of Homeland Security, U.S. Immigration and Customs Enforcement, Michael Garcia *Statement of Assistant Secretary Michael J. Garcia U.S. Immigration and Customs Enforcement Department of Homeland Security Before Senate Banking, Housing and Urban Affairs Committee on "9/11 Commission Report: Terrorist Financing Issues".* Washington, D.C.: September 29, 2004.

RAND Corporation. Nora Bensahel testimony before the House Armed Services Committee, Subcommittee on Oversight and Investigations. *International Perspectives on Interagency Reform.* January 29, 2008. 114.

The White House, Office of the Press Secretary, For Immediate Release *Remarks by the President on Security Reviews,* January 05, 2010. Washington D.C. (accessed at http://www.whitehouse.gov/the-press-office/remarks-president-security-reviews on January 12, 2010).

The White House, Office of the Press Secretary, For Immediate Release: R*emarks by the President on a New Strategy for Afghanistan and Pakistan,* March 27, 2009. Washington D.C.:2009. (accessed at http://www.whitehouse.gov/ the_press_office/ remarks-by-the-president-on-a-new-strategy-for-afghanistan-and-pakistan/ on January 12, 2010).

The White House, Office of the Press Secretary, For Immediate Release: Release *Remarks by the President on Security Reviews*, January 05, 2010. Washington D.C. (accessed at http://www.whitehouse.gov/the_press_office/remarks-by-the-president-on-a-new-strategy-for-afghanistan-and-pakistan/ on January 12, 2010).

U.S. Department of Homeland Security. *Statement by U.S. Department of Homeland Security Secretary Janet Napolitano on the Threat of Right-Wing Extremism,* Janet Napolitano, Office of the Press Secretary for the Department of Homeland Security, Washington D.C.,2009.

United States, News Release, *Three Al Qaeda Associates Arrested on Drug and Terrorism Charges*. DEA Acting Administrator Michele Leonhart and United States Attorney Preet Bharara. DEA Public Affairs Office. Washington D.C.: 2009.

United States. *Narco-Terrorism: International Drug Trafficking and Terrorism, a Dangerous Mix : Hearing Before the Committee on the Judiciary, United States Senate, One Hundred Eighth Congress, First Session, May 20, 2003*. Washington, D. C.: U.S. G.P.O., 2003.

United States. Statement for Immediate release, *Sahim Alwan Sentenced for Providing Material Support to Al Qaeda.* Department of Justice, www.USDOJ.gov Washington D.C.: 2003. (accessed at http://www.fbi.gov/dojpressrel/pressrel03/ sahim121703.htm, January 10,2010).

APPENDIX I: DHS STRATEGIC PLAN: FUNCTIONALITIES

Intelligence Fusion is the timely and advanced sharing of information between members of the HS community of interest (COI). It is also the determination of collection requirements based on imminent and emerging threats and the volatile security environment. Pertinent collection and timely distribution of information and intelligence has been a weakness, pointed out repeatedly, in security failures since 9/11 through the failed terrorist bombing attempt of a Christmas day, 2009, transatlantic flight to Detroit, MI. Exploitation of intelligence sharing gaps and systemic failures at seams in screening procedures, made the attempt possible. Synthesis and real-time distribution of intelligence saves lives, reduces cost and assist in foiling terrorist attempts that will alleviate the need for across the board reactive actions and increased use of response resources. The IA supporting functions of information sharing, international security cooperation and cross-functional jurisdiction are essential to providing HS collaboration. This thesis avoids extensive analysis of HS/HD intelligence deficiencies as they are not within the proposed scope of this thesis.

Border Security and Transportation Protection is protection from the transnational threat to the U.S. from the entry of contraband material, narcotics and human smuggling organizations, and the susceptibility of trafficking organizations to exploitation by violent extremists. As it pertains to threat assessment of critical vulnerabilities, protecting the U.S. mass transportation systems have become a major HS function. Transportation safety was moved to the forefront of the global terrorism stage as a consequence of 9/11.

Domestic Terrorism is inclusive of the investigation, apprehension, and prosecution of terrorists that could compromise U.S. and community of interest (COI)[1] security and safety. Government counter-actions dictate programs to detect, disrupt, and destroy internal and external terrorist organization support networks, and safe havens. Domestic terrorism now includes U.S. citizens who have become ideological converts, the result of extremist seeds sown 3000 miles away and reaped locally in the form of violence on U.S. soil. The use of strategic communications that normally target enemy participants, surrounding populations and the community of interest (COI), have added a new dimension to the Al Qaida Information Operations (IO): U.S. citizen converts. The investigation of U.S. citizens connected to extremist organizations, the exploitation of trans-national financial mechanisms and the incidents narco-terrorists uniting with extremists for profits also present new law enforcement challenges that require collaboration and alliances to manage creatively.

---

[1] The community of interest (COI) refers to the stakeholders at all levels of Homeland Security and subsequently National Security. It is better described as a national enterprise on page viii of the 2010 Department of Homeland Security Quadrennial Homeland Security Review: *"the term connotes a broad-based community with a common interest in the public safety and well-being of America and American society that is composed of multiple actors and stakeholders whose roles and responsibilities are distributed and shared."*

APPENDIX I: DHS STRATEGIC PLAN: FUNCTIONALITIES

Critical Infrastructure and Key Resource Protection is the protection of, mitigation of and recovery from attacks against vital U.S. cultural, business and governmental networks. A comprehensive security effort must enlist the IA, NGO and the COI collaboratively in order to identify threats, vulnerabilities, and develop response and recovery protocols that work. The enemy has shown us that centers of gravity (CoG) are no longer only military or government locations, and that symbolic strikes at cultural, political or economic icons will produce the manifestation of fear and the inducement of panic in a population, which will affect all aspects of a nation's demeanor.

Weapons of Mass Destruction (WMD) was originally considered a non-proliferation function enforced through diplomacy, deterrence and sanctions. This duty has evolved to include recovery and rehabilitation phases providing for the capability of national resources to prepare for, respond to and recover from the illicit use of Chemical, Biological, Radiological, Nuclear and, High Yield Explosives (CBRNE). The evolving ability of non-state actors to acquire and deliver a catastrophic strike now requires a domestic response mechanism equal to that threat. DoD resources include robust CBRNE response capabilities. DHS through its use of grants and training has developed improved domestic CBRNE capabilities, however the ability of the U.S. Government to respond effectively to domestic events remains minimal and is still evolving.

Emergency Preparedness and Continuity of Government- refers to the preparation for crisis response and consequence management of naturally or un-naturally initiated catastrophic events. The 9/11 attacks awakened America to the need for protection of vital government infrastructure. DHS is also responsible for the development and implementation of the National Response Framework (NRF), National Incident Management System (NIMS) and the Incident Command System (ICS) to facilitate a rapid return to normalcy following a catastrophic event. The scope of resiliency following catastrophic events requires teamwork from government and non-government entities, as the American people are the stakeholders, enlisting their aid ensures understanding of actions, economy of effort and unity of purpose. DoD and DHS through national, state and local level exercises realizes continual review and critical evaluation of the NRF. There is however a disparity between the military and IA critical incident exercise systems, which exposes a vital deficiency in the disaster response ability of the U.S. NS reform will require parity and cooperation between the incident exercise functions and encourage interoperability at all levels of domestic incident response.

APPENDIX II: US NORTHCOM COMPONENTS

NORTHCOM Functional Component Commands

Army North (ARNORTH) provides Defense Coordinating Officers (DCO) to Federal Emergency Management Agency (FEMA) regional offices throughout the U.S. DCOs coordinate DOD domestic support efforts during crisis response.

Air Force North (AFNORTH) holds the responsibility for NORTHCOM's air component duties. AFNORTH is also the U.S. portion of the bilateral Canadian and U.S. aircraft alert response mechanism for aerial defense, joint air surveillance and coordination with the Federal Aviation Administration (FAA).

Marine Forces North (MARFORNORTH) is responsible for force-protection of Marine installations in the NORTHCOM AOR. For domestic incident response purposes, the command provides Marine Emergency Preparedness Liaison Officers (EP-LNOs) focused on CS planning work in FEMA, DOD, and state operations centers to coordinate DoD Marine support.

US Navy Fleet Forces Command (USFF) While not a component sub-command of NORTHCOM, serves in a supporting role as the Joint Force Maritime Component Commander (JFMCC) for NORTHCOM, maintaining US coastal alert forces and providing maritime HD and Defense Support to Civil Authorities (DSCA) for humanitarian aid and disaster assistance.

Command/Control/Coordination

Standing Joint Forces Headquarters North (SJFHQ-N) SJFHQ-N is the NORTHCOM (C2) element for domestic contingency operations. SJFHQ-N's mission is command and control, situational awareness, mission coordination, and management of DoD resources in the NORTHCOM AOR.

Joint Interagency Coordination Group (JIACG). The JIACG is NORTHCOM's IA liaison unit, comprised of more than sixty HD COI agencies, The JIACG is the center of gravity for fusion of IA and DoD planning. The successful nature of the JIACG's structure is its unity of effort, which produces results through cooperation and cognizance of member equities.

Functional Task Forces

Joint Task Force North (JTF-N) JTF-N is the NORTHCOM/ law enforcement (LE) operations linchpin. JTF-N provides a wide breadth of reconnaissance, surveillance, detection, and infrastructure construction missions leveraging DoD training requirements for capabilities required by LE agencies with border protection and CNE duties. JTF-N was preceded by JTF-6, which primarily provided assistance to LE agencies with Counter Narcotics Enforcement (CNE) duties on the southwest border. JTF-N, in keeping with its HD duties, integrates military capabilities with federal, state and local law enforcement.

APPENDIX II: US NORTHCOM COMPONENTS

Functional Task Forces

Joint Task Force Civil Support (JTF-CS). This JTF assists the designated, lead federal agency in consequence management of domestic (inclusive of U.S. territories and possessions) chemical, biological, radiological, nuclear, or high-yield explosive events.

The JTF-CS national cadre primarily consists of state National Guard Bureau (NGB), Civil Support (CS) teams.

Geographic Task Forces

Joint Force Headquarters, National Capital Region (JFHQ-NCR) The JTFHQ-NCR coordinates joint planning, training, notional and practical exercises between DoD and the COI in the Washington D.C. vicinity

Joint Task Force Alaska (JTF-AK) coordinates land defense and DSCA in Alaska.

National Guard Bureau (NGB) NORTHCOM coordinates closely with the NGB, due to the capability of National Guard units to perform under state active duty authority directed by governors or to act under Title 32 as state directed federally compensated resources. Full-time, active duty, National Guardsmen are the primary work force which comprise the domestic Chemical, Biological, Radiological, Nuclear, high yield Explosive (CBRNE) and Civil Support Teams (CS). NGB personnel also serve in staff positions within NORTHCOM. CS teams perform primary assessment and coordination of military assistance to civil authorities following catastrophic events to determine and coordinate consequence-management (CM) response such as CBRNE teams. CBRNE units are trained to respond to domestic catastrophic events (natural or man-made) and in concert with stakeholder responders, support containment, recovery and resilience efforts in that regard. The National Defense Authorization Act of 2008 upgraded the NGB Chief to a four star general and designated the NGB as a DoD joint activity, validating the contribution of the NGB as integral to the comprehensive HD/HS effort.

APPENDIX III: DHS OPERATION CENTERS

DHS, Customs and Border Protection (CBP) administers two multi-agency operations centers under DHS purview; the National Targeting Center (NTC- passenger and cargo) and the Air and Marine Operations Center (AMOC).

National Targeting Center (NTC): The NTC continually monitors the international movement of potential terrorists and materials of interest verifying inquiries and coordinating operational level anti-terrorism response and law enforcement (LE) support detection of possible breach entry attempts. The NTC serves as a single point of reference for DHS screening and, targeting duties and support of all agency field-level anti-terrorism activities by providing tactical targeting and analytical research. NTC serves as a single point of reference for all agency anti-terrorism efforts.

Air and Marine Operations Center (AMOC) coordinates with NORAD to maintain situational awareness, coordinates integrated interdiction of U. S. airspace and marine border incursions, surveillance of border general aviation, and sea-lanes, to identify and in security verification of air and marine craft transiting U.S. areas of interest. AMOC is supported and supporting to NORAD.

Transportation Security Operations Center (TSOC) The Transportation Security Administration (TSA) manages its own operations center to monitor worldwide commercial transportation functions. TSA Operations Center, Command Watch is responsible for coordinating U.S. incident management for commercial transit (air, sea, bus, and rail) to facilitate investigation, prevention response, and recovery from threats or catastrophic events of associated U.S. infrastructure.

Besides the TSA Command Watch, the TSOC comprises two additional watch functions— **National Capital Region Coordination Center (NCRCC)**, which is responsible for air security and defense functions within the National Capitol Region; and the **National Infrastructure Coordination Center (NICC)**, which monitors the nation's critical infrastructure and key resources. The TSOC also houses the TSA **Mission Operations Center (MOC)**, which coordinates Federal Air Marshall (FAM) airspace law-enforcement functions.

National Operations Center Inter-agency Watch (NOC): DHS's Operations Directorate directs the efforts of the National Operations Center (NOC) interagency watch, a 24-hour collaborative construct that monitors U.S. information and intelligence of developing events.

APPENDIX IV: SWOT ANALYSIS

Opportunities

Opportunities	HSC/DHS	NSC/DOD	
COLLABORATION WITH STATE AND LOCALS PROMOTES ADDITIONAL STRUCTURES OR TO SECURITY SPHERE STRUCTURE	Y	N	COLLABORATION
ELIMINATION OF REPLICATED ISSUES/ MISSION REDUCES ISSUE/OF AMBIGUITY AND VULNERABILITY	Y	Y	COOPERATION
EXPAND KNOWLEDGE AND RESILIENCE/ BASE OF INFORMING HS CADRE THROUGH EDUCATION AND JOINT BILLETS OF CIVILIAN MILITARY AND OGA	Y	Y	INFORMATION / RESEARCH REDUCATIONAL ENHANCEMENTS
DIVERSITY IN VERTICAL PROMOTES COLLATERAL EXPERTISE FOR RECONSTRUCTION AND STABILITY RELATED EFFORTS OCCURS	Y	Y	INNOVATION EXPANSION
EXECUTION LEGAL DIRECTED COORDINATION WILL PROVIDE SOURCING CONTROL OF SUPPLY ACTIVITIES VERTICAL INTEGRATION	Y	Y	VERTICAL INTEGRATION
GLOBAL COMMONS ACCESS IS SUPPORTIVE OF CT AND CHE AS THREAT EXPANDS	Y	Y	GLOBAL SECURITY COOPERATION
MERGING OF TRANSNATIONAL CRIMINAL ACTIVITY WITH TERRORIST ACTIVITIES PROVIDES ADDITIONAL OPPORTUNITIES FOR STRONGER APPLICATION OF COLLECT AND ONE CAPABILITIES (ATTACKS)	Y	Y	EXPLOITATION OF ENEMY CRITICAL VULNERABILITY
THE THREAT ENVIRONMENT IS GROWING IN DIVERSITY AND SPEED CAUSING ADVERSARIAL ELEMENTS TO RELY MORE ON TECHNOLOGY WHICH IS MORE EASILY EXPLOITED BY AGENCIES	Y	Y	THREAT ENVIRONMENT GROWTH
LEGAL ENHANCEMENTS FOR INVESTIGATION OF TERRORISM AND TRANSNATIONAL CRIMINAL ACTIVITY (PATRIOT ACT, FISA AND INFRA CON) PROVIDE BETTER TOOLS FOR COMPREHENSIVE RESPONSE EFFORTS	Y	Y	LEGAL ENHANCEMENTS

Threats

Threats	HSC/DHS	NSC/DOD	
NON STATE ACTORS FUNDING INCREASING	Y	Y	WMD
THE DOMESTIC THREAT IS GROWING MORE RAPIDLY AND THAN EXPECTED	Y	Y	DOMESTIC THREAT GROWTH
ADVERSE SHIFTS IN FOREIGN ACTORS, NATION STATE ALLIANCES AND FOREIGN POLICY AFFECTING ECONOMIC ENVIRONMENT & AND OR TRADE POLICIES	Y	Y	ECONUS ENVIRONMENT
LEGAL/REGULATORY REQUIREMENTS ARE BECOMING ONEROUS TOWARD ACTION	Y	Y	REGULATORY RESTRICTIONS
VULNERABLE TO CHANGES IN THE DEFICIT AND RECESSION	Y	Y	BUDGET ISSUES
TERRORISM AND NARCO-TERRORISM ARE MERGING INTO A GREATER THREAT GIVING ADVERSARIES AN ADVANTAGE IN BOTH RESOURCES AND DIVERSITY OF EFFORTS	Y	Y	THREAT MERGE AND GROWTH= POWER
THREAT CHANGING IN DIRECTIONS THAT POINT AWAY FROM CURRENT ORGANIZATIONAL EXPERTISE	Y	Y	RESPONSE CAPABILITY
CHANGING FROM STRUCTURED ACTIVITY INTO A DECENTRALIZED MOVEMENT WITH SMALL GROUPS SELF-ORGANIZE TO CARRY OUT ATTACKS	Y	Y	DECENTRALIZED THREAT
DEMOGRAPHIC CHANGES IN IDEOLOGICAL POPULATIONS ARE HAVING A NEGATIVE IMPACT ON ORGANIZATIONAL STRATEGIC COMMUNICATIONS	Y	Y	DEMOGRAPHICS
TECHNOLOGY CAN CHANGE THE THREAT PICTURE WITHOUT WARNING	Y	Y	TECHNOLOGY

Y=Yes, Organization has that attribute

N=No, Organization does not have that attribute

HSC/DHS AND NSC/DOD-NORTHCOM SWOT ANALYSIS

Strengths

Strengths	HS/DHS	NSC/DOD	
HIGH LEVELS OF COMPETENCE	Y	Y	COMPETENCE
DIVERSE SKILL SET	Y	Y	COMPETITIVE SKILL
EXPERIENCE CURVE	N	Y	EXPERIENCE CURVE
ADEQUATE FINANCIAL RESOURCES	N	Y	FINANCIAL RESOURCES
REPUTATION	N	Y	REPUTATION
ACKNOWLEDGED LEADERSHIP IN THE DISCIPLINE	N	Y	LEADERSHIP
WELL-CONCEIVED FUNCTIONAL AREAS	N	Y	AG-NSC ORGANIZATIONAL RESPONSE
ACCESS TO ECONOMIES OF SCALE	N	Y	ECONOMIES OF SCALE
VERTICAL INTEGRATION	N	Y	IMPLEMENTATION EFFECTIVENESS
STRONG MANAGEMENT	N	Y	MANAGEMENT
SUPERIOR TECHNOLOGICAL/TECHNICAL SKILLS	Y	Y	TECHNICAL SKILLS
JURISDICTIONAL ADVANTAGE	Y	N	CROSS-FUNCTIONALITY

Weaknesses

Weaknesses	HSC/DHS	NSC/DOD	
CLEAR STRATEGIC DIRECTION DUE TO LACK OF CURRENT ISS	Y	Y	STRATEGY
FACILITIES ARE OBSOLETE AND ORGANIZATIONAL LEADERSHIP IS DECENTRALIZED	Y	N	FACILITIES
LACKING MANAGERIAL DEPTH AND TALENT	Y	N	MANAGEMENT
INTER-AGENCY COMPETITION	Y	Y	COMPETITIVE PRESSURE
MISSING KEY CAPABILITIES AND CAPACITIES	Y	Y	KEY CAPABILITIES
POOR TRACK RECORD IN IMPLEMENTING POLICY REPLACEMENT	Y	N	POLICY IMPLEMENTATION IS REACTIVE
WE ARE PLAGUED WITH HIGH PROFILE INTERNAL OPERATING PROBLEMS	Y	N	INTERNAL OPERATIONS
FALLING BEHIND ON RESEARCH & DEVELOPMENT	Y	N	R&D
LIMITED RESOURCES IN SPECIALTY RESPONSE CAPABILITIES	Y	Y	
WE HAVE A WEAK IMAGE	Y	N	IMAGE

Y=Yes, Organization has that attribute. N=No, Organization does not have that attribute

HSC/DHS AND NSC/DOD-NORTHCOM SWOT ANALYSIS

APPENDIX V: NATIONAL SECURITY STAFF STRUCTURE

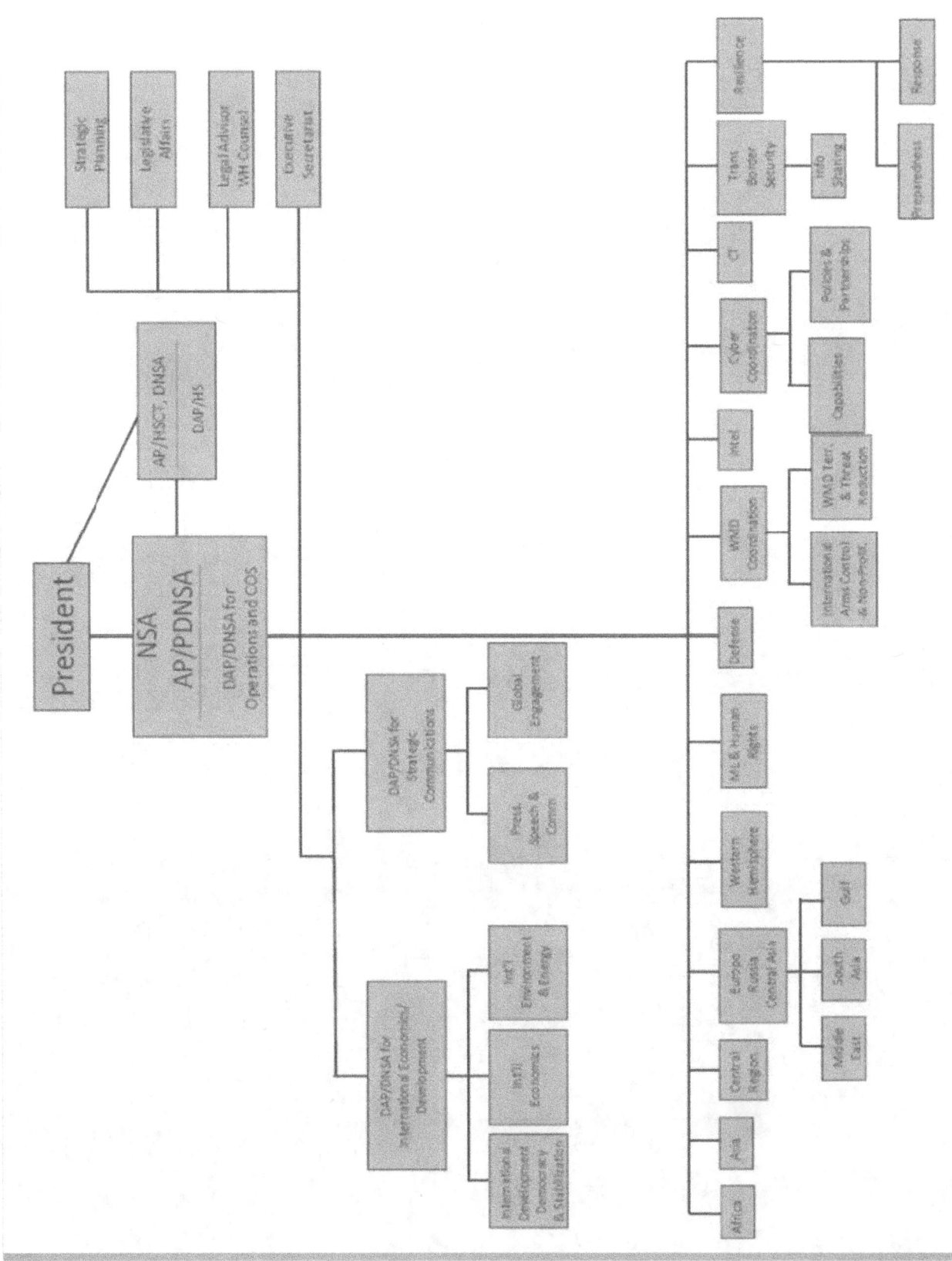

www.ingramcontent.com/pod-product-compliance
Lightning Source LLC
Chambersburg PA
CBHW081834280526
45789CB00007B/2453